MOORCROFT

William Moorcroft and Walter Moorcroft

MOORCROFT

A Guide to Moorcroft Pottery 1897–1993

Paul Atterbury

Additional material by Beatrice Moorcroft

Published by Richard Dennis & Hugh Edwards
The Old Chapel, Shepton Beauchamp, Somerset

Acknowledgements

This revised edition of *Moorcroft Pottery* replaces the out-of-print 1990 edition. The original text has been amended and several new interesting photographs have been included. A new section has been added bringing the history of design at Moorcroft up-to-date, including the 1993 additions to the ranges etc. The marks page has likewise been updated.

A special debt of gratitude is owed to W. Moorcroft PLC and members of the Moorcroft family for the loan of splendid pieces, for their acceptance of our many raids on family archives and the invasion of their privacy following hijacks of their houses as photographic studios.

To Walter, the Master Potter, and his wife Elisabeth, Managing Director John and his wife Gill, the late Mrs. Hazel Moorcroft, widow of William, and Beatrice, custodian of family records, we extend our warmest thanks. Of the many collectors who entrusted us with their pieces a special debt of gratitude is due to Mr. & Mrs. T.J. Archer, Maureen and Terry Batkin, Drs. A. and M. Belton, Michael Bruce, Cannonhall Museum, Barnsley, Rita and Robert Edgar-Dimmack, Mrs. V.H. Edwards, Mr. G.B. Habib, Ray Heath, Mr. and Mrs. J.R. Johnson, Liga Markley and Craig G. Myers, Haydn and Christine Miles, Bill and Margaret Munn, the Newstead family, Mr. and Mrs. J. Playfoot, Peter Rose, Mr. and Mrs. Clive Saych, Ian and Rita Smythe and above all, Barbara Tobias and Mr. and Mrs. Albert Wade.

For providing new photographs for this edition we wish to thank John McGhie, Rumours Decorative Arts, David Sampietro, Mrs. Ruth Simon, Graham Soal and the late Mr. Donald Watkin. Our thanks also go to Pru Cuming for performing miracles with her travelling photographic studio.

Photography: Prudence Cuming Associates, Michael Bruce at Gate Studios, Angela Coombes, O's Gallery Tokyo, Phillips and Sotheby's

Production: Wendy Wort

Print Design and Reproduction: Flaydemouse, Yeovil, England

© Paul Atterbury, Richard Dennis and Hugh Edwards

Published in 1990 by Richard Dennis and Hugh Edwards,
The Old Chapel, Shepton Beauchamp, Somerset TA19 0LE, England

Revised edition 1993. Reprinted 1996, 1998 & 2002.

A catalogue record for this book is available from the British Library

ISBN 0 903685 33 7

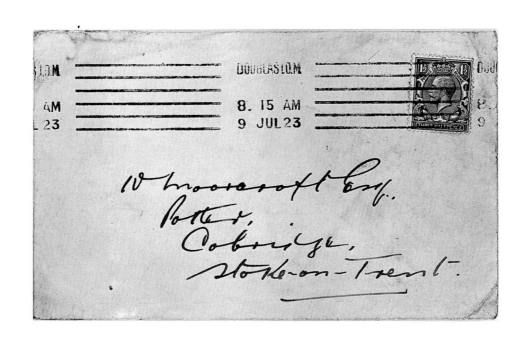

The Moorcroft pottery is located at Cobridge, on the Sandbach Road, Burslem, Stoke-on-Trent ST6 2DQ
Telephone Stoke-on-Trent (01782) 214323

Contents

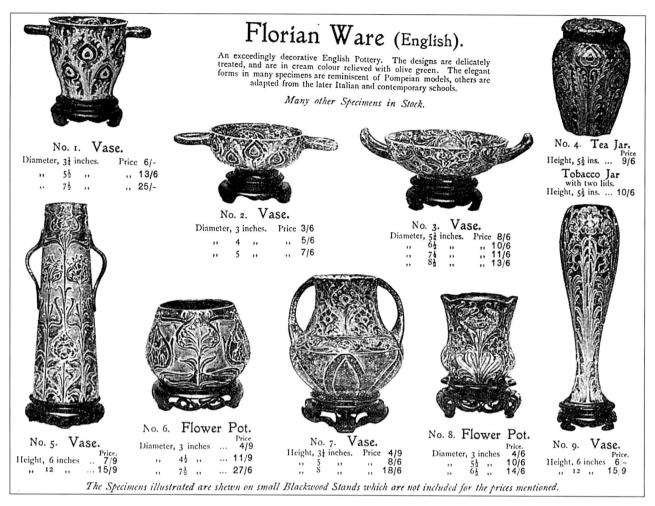

Florian Ware (English).

An exceedingly decorative English Pottery. The designs are delicately treated, and are in cream colour relieved with olive green. The elegant forms in many specimens are reminiscent of Pompeian models, others are adapted from the later Italian and contemporary schools.

Many other Specimens in Stock.

No. 1. Vase.
Diameter, 3½ inches.   Price 6/-
,,   5½ ,,   ,, 13/6
,,   7½ ,,   ,, 25/-

No. 2. Vase.
Diameter, 3 inches.   Price 3/6
,,   4 ,,   ,, 5/6
,,   5 ,,   ,, 7/6

No. 3. Vase.
Diameter, 5¼ inches.   Price 8/6
,,   6½ ,,   ,, 10/6
,,   7¼ ,,   ,, 11/6
,,   8¼ ,,   ,, 13/6

No. 4. Tea Jar.
Price
Height, 5½ ins. ... 9/6
Tobacco Jar
with two lids.
Height, 5½ ins. ... 10/6

No. 5. Vase.
Price.
Height, 6 inches .. 7/9
,,   12 ,,   ...15/9

No. 6. Flower Pot.
Price
Diameter, 3 inches ...   4/9
,,   4½ ,,   ... 11/9
,,   7½ ,,   ... 27/6

No. 7. Vase.
Height, 3½ inches.   Price 4/9
,,   5 ,,   ,, 8/6
,,   8 ,,   ,, 18/6

No. 8. Flower Pot.
Price.
Diameter, 3 inches   4/6
,,   5½ ,,   10/6
,,   6½ ,,   14/6

No. 9. Vase.
Price.
Height, 6 inches 6/-
,,   12 ,, 15/9

The Specimens illustrated are shewn on small Blackwood Stands which are not included for the prices mentioned.

1 Advertisement for Florian Ware from Liberty's Yule-Tide Gifts catalogue of 1901

2 Advertisement for Burslem Ware from Liberty's Yule-Tide Gifts catalogue of 1902

Burslem Ware (English).

Special attention is directed to the rich and decorative value of this new and effective English Pottery, which combines great beauty of form with originality and quaintness of decoration. The designs are produced in deep shades of blues and greens, upon a groundwork of rich grey-blue, relieved by an overglaze of yellow. For Overmantels and Sideboards

No. 1. Vase.
Height, 6 ins. Price, 8/6
Height, 9 ,,   ,, 16/6
Height, 12 ,,   ,, 25/-.

No. 2. Bowl.
Extreme diameter, 7 ins. Price, 12/6.

No. 3. Vase.
Height, 6½ ins. Price, 8/9
Height, 9 ,,   ,, 16/6.
Height, 14 ,,   ,, 30/-

No. 4. Vase.
Height, 8 ins. Price, 12/6.
Height, 10 ,,   ,, 16/6.
Height, 16 ,,   ,, 35/-.

No. 5. Vase.
Height, 6 ins. Price, 6/6
Height, 8 ,,   ,, 8/6.
Height, 10 ,,   ,, 15/6.
Height, 12 ,,   ,, 18/6.

No. 6. Vase.
Height, 7½ ins. Price, 10/6.

No. 7. Vase.
Height, 6 ins. Price, 7/9.
Height, 12½ ,,   ,, 25/-.

No. 8. Vase.
Height, 6½ ins. Price, 11/6.

Chapter One
William Moorcroft, 1872-1945

William Moorcroft was born in Burslem in 1872, the second son of a family well established in the Potteries. His father, Thomas, after training at Hanley and Burslem Schools of Art from 1863, had developed a considerable reputation as a designer and china painter, specialising in flower subjects. For some years he worked at the Hill Pottery, Burslem, with E J D Bodley. On 27 March 1869 he married Teresa Edge, a school governess, at the Wesleyan Methodist Church, Burslem, and over the next ten years they had six children, four of whom, all sons, survived childhood. Young William enjoyed a conventionally happy family life until 1881, when his mother Teresa died, aged 32. He and his brothers were then brought up by their father, with the help of their nurse Betsy, a girl of nineteen who, in March 1884, became their step-mother. Unfortunately, family life was again disrupted less than a year later with the sudden death of Thomas in January 1885.

Family difficulties do not seem to have hindered William Moorcroft's development. From the age of seven he had attended the Burslem Endowed School, first at the Wedgwood Institute, and then from 1880 in its new and palatial premises at Longport Hall, formerly the seat of the Davenport family. William appears to have been a good student, winning his first school prize at the age of eight. His early interest in art showed that he had inherited his father's talents, and by the age of twelve he was already attending art and design classes at the Wedgwood Institute. In later years William was to become a noted 'former student' of the Institute, his name being mentioned particularly in the annual prize giving address in 1904, following his success at the St Louis International Exhibition of that year. His youngest brother Harold, born in 1879, followed in his footsteps and became a gifted artist. For some years during the early 1900s he was General Manager of Marsden Tiles where he also designed a small range of art wares with graffito, or incised slip decoration, some of which he signed. Soon after 1912 he moved to the United States, remaining there until his retirement in 1928 or 1930. (For further details of William's early life, see Beatrice Moorcroft's article, *Growing up in Burslem*, in Newsletter 2, 1989, of the Moorcroft Collectors' Club.)

In 1895 William was studying at the National Art Training School in South Kensington, later the Royal College of Art. He not only attended the usual lectures and classes but embarked on an intensive study of ancient and modern pottery and porcelain at the British Museum and the South Kensington Museum, a course of study he later pursued further in Paris. By 1897 he had obtained his Art Master's Certificate, the ultimate goal of every student of the government schools of art. This would have enabled him to earn his living by teaching, but he had set his heart on a career as a potter. His opportunity to realise his ambition arose when he was offered a job as a designer by the china and earthenware manufacturers, James Macintyre & Company of the Washington Works, Burslem.

Macintyre's, a large and influential company established in Burslem since the late 1830s, had made their name as manufacturers of a wide range of commercial pottery and porcelain, which included advertising ashtrays and other similar specialities, commemorative wares, door furniture and other architectural fittings, artists' palettes, tiles and chemical and sanitary wares, as well as tablewares. Their output was largely utilitarian, but their

3 Thrower and assistant at the Macintyre Works c1900. William Moorcroft, wearing bowler hat, looks on

3a The Macintyre Works c1900, turner and assistant at the lathe. In the foreground, unturned pots. On the left, turned pots and two decorated examples

standards were high. Llewellyn Jewitt, in his book *The Ceramic Art of Great Britain* (1884) had commended Macintyre's for their technical achievements, which included an ivory china used, among other things, for the backs of hairbrushes and hand mirrors, a range of decorative clay bodies imitating agate, malachite and other natural materials, and special glazes such as a glossy black jet. This, developed first for door furniture and inkstands and often enriched with enamels and gilding, was in use throughout the Potteries by the end of the century for the manufacture of inexpensive teapots. James Macintyre had died in 1868, and the company had then come under the control of Thomas Hulme and William Woodall. The latter, Chairman until 1893, was also a local Member of Parliament for twenty years, and his brother Corbett who succeeded him as Chairman then masterminded a considerable expansion of the Washington Works, aided by the Managing Director Henry Watkin. The making of tableware, in production since the early 1880s, was greatly enlarged, and included both printed and painted porcelain and earthenwares decorated by dipping in coloured slips, mostly greens, pinks and browns. In 1889 they began to experiment with porcelain insulators and switchgear for the new electricity industry, pioneer work that was to produce results upon which Macintyre's future came to depend. The policy of expansion created a company employing up to 400 people by the early 1900s.

Part of this expansion had been the decision, in 1893, to develop a range of ornamental art pottery. Art pottery had by this time become a vogue, a direct legacy of William Morris and the Aesthetic Movement. Companies, large and small, were busily introducing new art ranges, and advertisements which emphasised 'art' in the crudest terms littered the pages of magazines such as the *Pottery Gazette*. In 1899, the editor of the *Magazine of Art* felt compelled to comment: 'There has been of late years such a large production of so called "art pottery" that (it) has almost become a term of reproach, whether regarded from the point of view of design or decoration . . .'

Undeterred by such competition, Macintyre's determined to excel in the field, and began to search for a designer capable of developing the new ware. Between 1893 and 1895 they appear to have engaged a succession of artists and modellers whose careers at the factory were short. Several were engaged on a trial basis, among them a Mr Scaife, of whose work little is known and Mr Rowley who specialised in lustre ware. In 1894 the firm was able to participate in the *Exhibition of Decorative and Artistic Pottery* held in London at the Imperial Institute and to show examples of their ware alongside that of Doulton, Minton, Ault, Sir Edmond Elton and other well established manufacturers of art pottery. Their exhibits included tableware designed by Richard Lunn and two types of decorative slipware known as Taluf Ware and Washington Faience. Of these, the former displayed a type of slip decoration with patterns cut through layers of coloured slip on a lathe or by hand, while the latter was a kind of sprigged ware, with relief ornament by Mr Wildig, 'gold medallist of South Kensington'. Wildig was a local artist and modeller, who had studied in the Potteries before going to South Kensington. He was a successful artist craftsman who had gained a number of medals, including the rare and much coveted gold medal in the National Competitions held annually by the Department of Science and Art. He was employed by Macintyre's for several years but finally left to set up his own studio in Hanley.

Macintyre's had been among the more generous supporters of the Burslem School of Art and had shown a preference for local talent, but in 1894 they looked further afield and, at the suggestion of the Chairman and Gilbert Redgrave, they invited Harry Barnard to leave London to take over the design and production of an entirely new art pottery, that was to be decorated in 'plastic clay'. Barnard had been trained as a modeller at Fulham and had worked at Doulton's Lambeth studio, initially as an assistant to Mark V. Marshall, and later in his own right. He joined Macintyre's in February 1895, on a two year agreement, and started to develop a

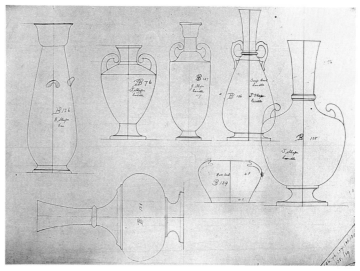

4 During his brief stay at the Washington Works, Harry Barnard produced a large number of shape designs, relating to many areas of Macintyre production. Many may not have been produced, but the drawings do reveal his interest in classical, Middle Eastern and Far Eastern forms, sources that were subsequently developed further by Moorcroft

5 Few of Barnard's designs for decoration survive from his time at Macintyre's, but those that do suggest that Moorcroft may well have made use of them when designing his Aurelian Wares, as well as the Dura tableware and some early Florian patterns

6 Design for a salad bowl, typical of the many shape designs carried out by Moorcroft early in his career at the Washington Works

7 Macintyre invoice dated May 31, 1910, relating to the sale of red and green Claremont Pompeian bowls to Liberty's

form of *pâte sur pâte*, adapting to a more commercial method of production the expensive low-relief slip modelling technique associated since the early 1870s with Louis Marc Solon and the Minton factory. Painting in coloured slip was, in any case, a well-established method of decoration in the pottery industry and many factories had practised the French-inspired Barbotine technique since the 1860s. Barnard described his process, which in some ways resembled gesso, or plaster work, in his Personal Record, an unpublished memoir written in 1931. He called it a kind of '*pâte sur pâte* modelling' but the secret was a modelling tool of his own design. He wrote, 'This proved to be quite a surprise, nothing like it had ever been seen before. To make it a commercial line, I introduced an appliqué slip in the form of a stencil pattern, and the slip modelling was a freehand treatment and covered up the spaces necessary in the stencil pattern, and so hid to a great extent that it was applied in that way . . .' Barnard's high relief flowing designs, which blended both Art Nouveau and revived Rococo or 18th century elements, were launched by Macintyre's under the name of Gesso Faience and were marked with a special printed backstamp. Barnard had his own workshops and a staff of girl decorators, and there was considerable investment in the new venture. However, the new range was only partially successful and the relationship between Barnard and Macintyre's Managing Director, Henry Watkin became increasingly strained. In February 1897, at the end of his two-year agreement, Barnard left to start a far more successful career with Wedgwood, for whom he had already been working for two days a week.

It is a temptation to dismiss Harry Barnard's work with Macintyre's as a period of minor importance but in fact his achievements during this time were considerable and had a direct bearing on subsequent developments at the Washington Works. He claimed that over a hundred of his designs went into production, mostly for the decoration of domestic wares such as teapots, jugs, tobacco-jars, inkpots, salad bowls and match stands. At the same time he created a wide range of tableware and ornamental shapes, many of which were produced. A notable example is an egg cup with individual salt and pepper in the form of bird's eggs, a design later taken over by Moorcroft. His surviving drawings from this period reveal his grasp of contemporary design ideas, and so his failure at Macintyre's was probably more the result of a clash of personalities than a lack of

creative ability. Indeed, his work could have been the source for some of William Moorcroft's early printed and slip-trailed patterns. However, Barnard's legacy was most important in the area of raised slip decoration, for it was he who introduced this technique to Macintyre's, and thus planted the seed that Moorcroft was to cultivate so successfully. While the actual technique is different, it is no accident that the thick and heavy slip-drawing on early Florian Wares does resemble Gesso Faience. Apart from the obvious links between the two designers, their wares were, after all, produced in the same department, and by the same girls.

Towards the end of the Barnard period, the Macintyre directors had already begun to look for another designer, and they decided this time to revert to local talent. In March 1897 they appointed William Moorcroft to the post. Young ambitious, with firm ideas about design and decoration inspired by William Morris, and armed with the latest principles of design as taught at the Royal College of Art, Moorcroft had much to commend him as a designer. Unlike the majority of the art students trained in the government schools of art, he had also studied ceramic chemistry and had acquired experience of ceramic processes, qualifications that would enable him to execute his own designs or supervise their execution by others. During the first nine months that followed his appointment he introduced a new and original style of decoration for Macintyre's printed and enamelled ware, and designed new shapes and decoration for their plain coloured tablewares. For the printed and enamelled ware he designed shapes for both vases and domestic ware and decorated them with patterns consisting of highly conventionalised floral motifs, frets and diapers, in a fashion that owed more to the decorative traditions of Morris and the English designers than to continental Art Nouveau, with which his decoration has been compared. The new ware was given the name Aurelian and three of the designs were registered in February 1898. Having begun the development of Aurelian Ware, produced in Macintyre's main decorating room, Moorcroft turned his attention to the slipware. Macintyre's had been producing plain tableware that they called 'Tinted Faience' for some time, but Moorcroft introduced new shapes and colours that prepared the way for Dura Ware, for which he later became responsible. The plain surface invited decoration and Macintyre's had already introduced a range of tableware on which patterns were outlined in white slip by the process of slip trailing, or tube lining, a method of decoration used throughout the Potteries for the decoration of tiles. This range, marketed under the Gesso Faience backstamp, was probably part of the Barnard legacy. Moorcroft was quick to appreciate the possibilities of slip trailing and explored its potential to develop a new range. By the end of 1897, he had introduced a number of designs for tableware and the first ornamental pieces in what was to develop into his characteristic and highly individual style.

Early in 1898 Moorcroft was promoted to become Manager of the Ornamental Ware, and provided with his own workrooms, a staff of decorators and the services of a thrower and turner who would work exclusively for him. He was asked to develop a new range of decorative ware, using the technique of slip-trailing and underglaze colour that he had already begun to explore. The result was Florian Ware, a name indicative of the floral motifs that were the basis of most of the designs. A new backstamp was prepared, but the Gesso Faience mark outlived the ware for which it had been intended and continued in casual and occasional use on Florian Ware and Dura tableware for several years. This has confused subsequent generations of collectors, and explains why pieces have been recorded carrying both the Gesso Faience mark and Moorcroft's signature.

Moorcroft quickly developed his own design and working methods. Given sole responsibility for the development of Florian Ware, the training and supervision of his staff, and access to the firm's laboratories, clayrooms, dipping house and commercial kilns in which the ware was fired, he was able to control the design and manufacture of his ware from clay to kiln, and experiment

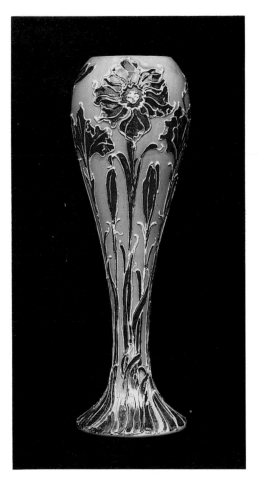
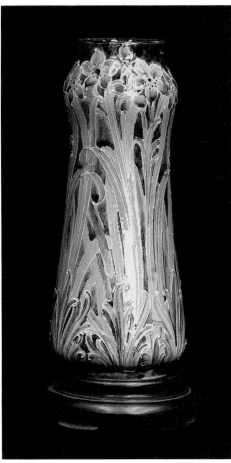

8 Nine prints taken from a collection of glass negatives, dating from the early 1900s and recently found in the factory, reveal a number of Florian Ware patterns some of which are previously unrecorded, along with some unusual shapes and styles of slip-trailing. Notable is the narrow necked vase below right, decorated with butterflies and sailing boats

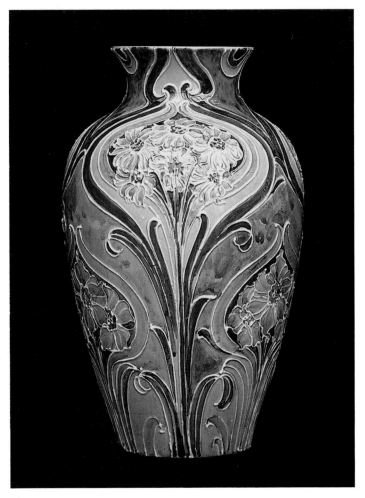

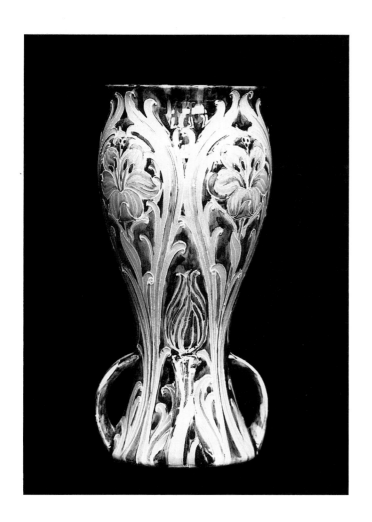
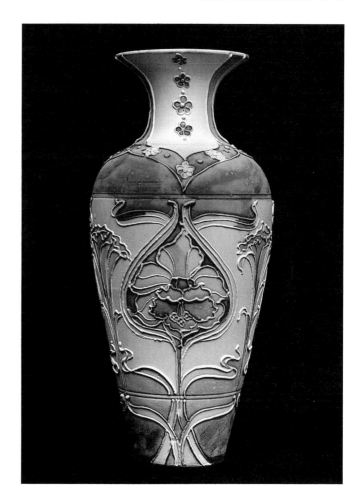
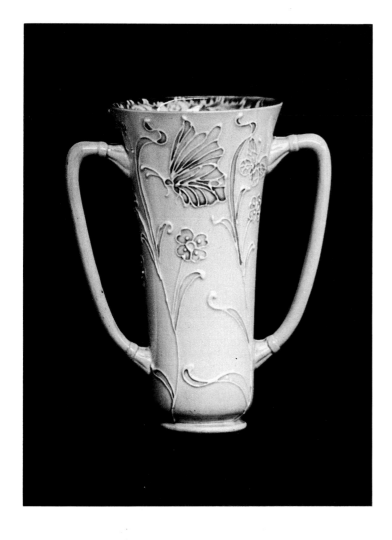
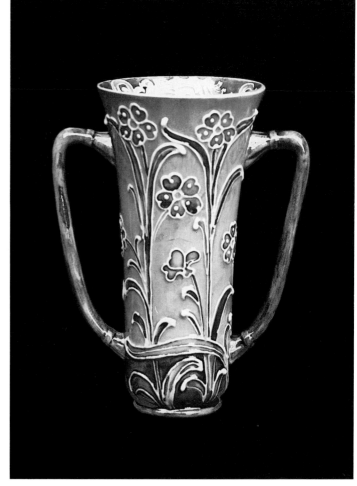

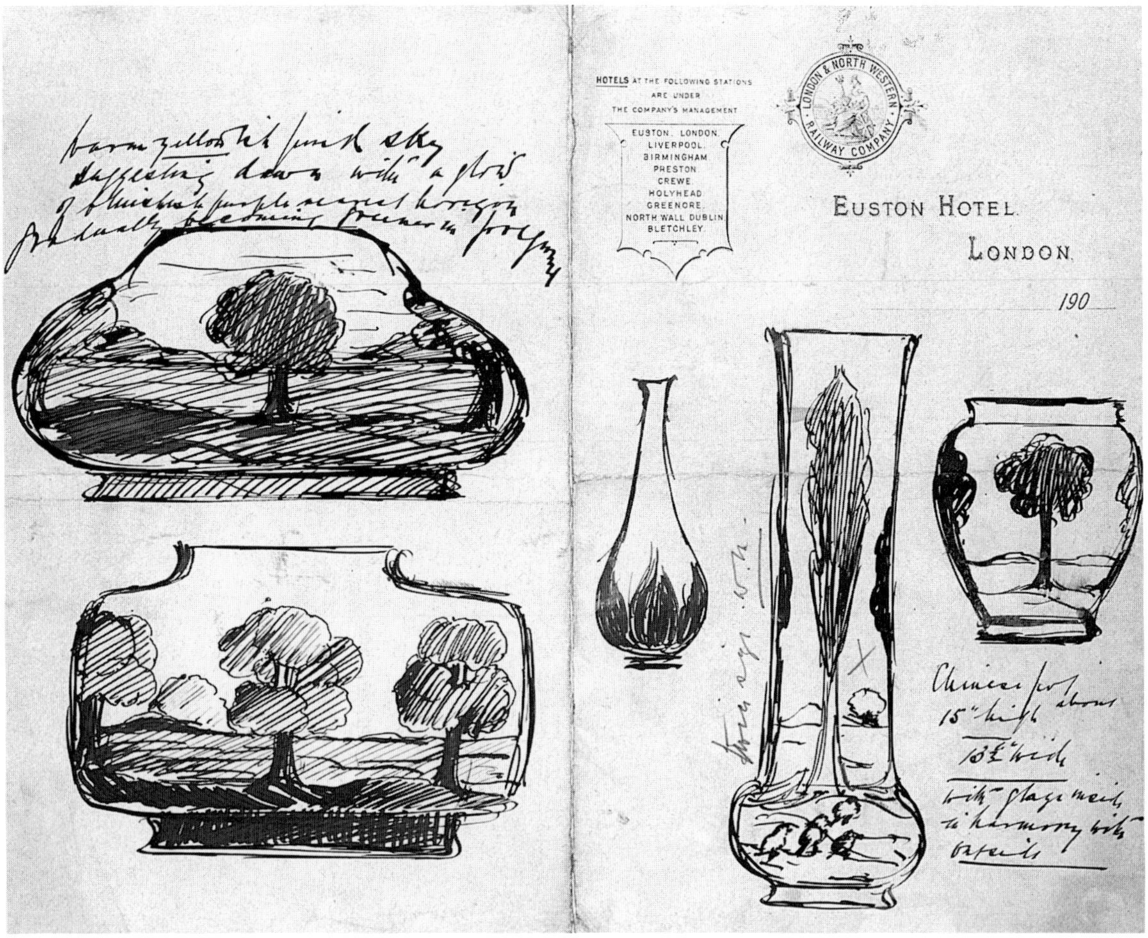
HOTELS AT THE FOLLOWING STATIONS
ARE UNDER
THE COMPANY'S MANAGEMENT
EUSTON, LONDON.
LIVERPOOL.
BIRMINGHAM.
PRESTON.
CREWE.
HOLYHEAD.
GREENORE.
NORTH WALL DUBLIN.
BLETCHLEY.
LONDON & NORTH WESTERN
RAILWAY COMPANY
EUSTON HOTEL.
LONDON.
190

9 Moorcroft drew constantly, on any scrap of paper that came to hand, but he seems to have preferred old invoices, envelopes and other people's stationery. These drawings, dating from the early 1900s, show sketches for landscape and banded vases, and tablewares

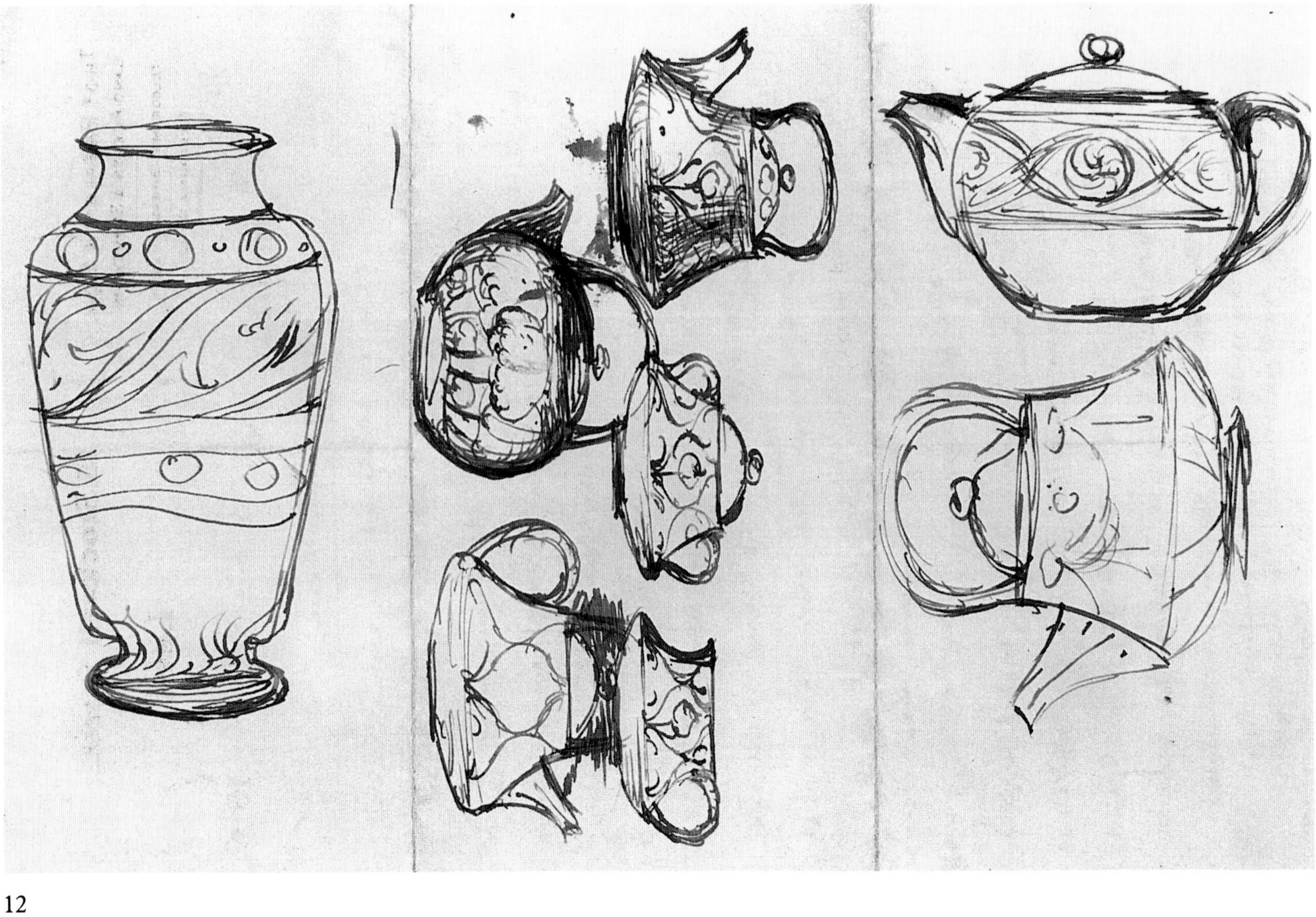

10 *The Moorcroft factory, photographed in 1930. The three bottle ovens, or kilns, on the right were still in use. The left hand one of the three was built in 1913 and was used for both the biscuit firings and the glost (glaze) firings. A second bottle oven was built next to it in 1915 when the factory was extended and in 1919 the third oven was added. This third oven, which is still standing today as a listed building, became the biscuit oven leaving the first two to be used only as glost ovens; they were demolished in 1956 to make room for the new electric kilns. The two chimneys to the left of the picture were muffle kilns – the nearer one being used for lustres and the other for flambé. They were built in 1919–20 and were demolished in 1971*

11 *A range of pomegranate pattern bowls for flower arrangement with Art Nouveau pewter and enamel bases, c 1912*

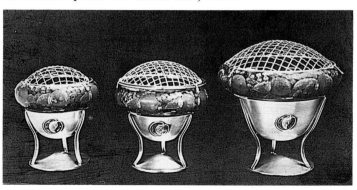

freely with colour, glaze and decorating techniques. He established a design philosophy that was to stay with him for the rest of his life. His early diaries reveal his interest in organic form; from plants he developed the principle that ornament should be used to emphasise form, and never for its own sake. In this he had more in common with Christopher Dresser than with many contemporary potters, such as William de Morgan, for whom decoration was of paramount importance. Like many English designers in the Arts and Crafts movement, who followed William Morris, Moorcroft disliked continental Art Nouveau, and described the more extreme characteristics of the style as 'a disease'. His concern for form gave him an uneasy relationship with the style, and his determination to link shape and decoration put him apart from the more extravagant aspects of Art Nouveau. In his use of slip trailing and a sinuous flowing style of decoration based on nature, Moorcroft can be included among the avante garde designers who introduced modern European styles into England.

Moorcroft's interest in form also lay behind his method of working. Whenever possible, all pieces were thrown on the wheel, to allow the pot to develop organically. He used a fine white porcellaneous body, developed by Macintyre's for industrial use and thus capable of withstanding high temperatures. Working in the round, Moorcroft drew the designs himself, adapting the patterns to fit every size and shape of pot. Assistants then outlined the designs with a fine extrusion of slip. This outline, drawn heavily on the early pieces, and gradually becoming almost imperceptible later, formed a cloisonnist pattern that created a relief effect. At the same time it served to separate the colours. These, derived from metallic oxides, were painted on underglaze and then each piece was fired at least twice to 1100 degrees centigrade or more. The final clear glaze was highly vitrified, emphasising the depth and richness of the colours. When Florian Ware was launched the colour range was restricted to blues, greens, pinks and yellow, but later Moorcroft was able to develop new underglaze colours capable of withstanding the high temperatures.

Moorcroft drew and controlled the design of every pattern executed in his department, including both ornamental and useful ware, and he was also responsible for many of the shapes. These reflect his wide-ranging interests, with forms drawn from Middle Eastern, Far Eastern and contemporary Art Nouveau styles. Also important was Classicism, and notably the influence of Roman ceramics excavated at Pompeii. An early factory photograph headed 'Reproductions of Pompeian Bowls & Vases found at Pompeii' shows nine shapes, all registered in 1900, made in up to six sizes, and all with Florian decoration. This influence was noted by the *Magazine of Art* in December 1900, and which said: 'Mr Moorcroft has set himself to adapt the shapes of the early Roman pottery to modern requirements and to decorate them with modern ornaments . . . and he has succeeded in no small measure . . .' Distinguished particularly by the flat handles, this style was present for many years and the word Pompeian occurs frequently on invoices and other factory documents, and was still in use as late as 1935. The thrower, turner and the decorators who worked with Moorcroft used their skills entirely under his direction. As a result, both the Florian Ware and the later ranges were the creation of one mind. Moorcroft's insistence upon retaining the responsibility for the design of every piece separates his work from that of the majority of English art potters with whom group, or studio, methods were commonplace. This method of working was seen by many as one of the particular qualities of Florian Ware and enabled Moorcroft to sign his work as his own, by signing his name or initials with a brush, laden with colour, or a wooden point, on the bottom of each piece. Contemporary magazines commented on the ware soon after its introduction, the *Studio* calling it 'the most interesting work in pottery executed entirely on the clay'. The *Magazine of Art* went further: 'One interesting feature of this ware is that it bears indelibly the mark of the artist and skilled craftsman. All the designs are the work of Mr W. Moorcroft; every piece is examined by him at each stage, and is revised and corrected as much as is necessary before being passed into the oven. The decorative work is executed by students – who have to go through a course of training at the Burslem Art Schools – and while the design of Mr Moorcroft is as closely followed as possible, any individual touches of the operators are seldom interfered with if they tend to improvement. It thus happens that no two pieces are individually alike . . . . . this ware deserves a large share of popularity. Messrs. Macintyre are to be congratulated on their success in placing before the public a ware that really exhibits evidence of thoughtful art and skilful craftsmanship.'

When Florian Ware was launched, many of the designs and some of the shapes were registered, maintaining a tradition established by Macintyre's long before Moorcroft joined the company. The first Florian designs were registered in September and October 1898, and other registrations then followed at regular intervals until April 1905. Florian Ware was quickly successful, and within a year of its introduction it was being sold by Liberty of London, Tiffany of New York and Rouard of Paris. The range in the process established Moorcroft's characteristic style and his reputation as a designer was enhanced by the considerable diversity of the Florian patterns. Formalised flower and plant forms predominated, with an emphasis on English flowers, for example poppies, bluebells, cornflowers, tulips, lilac, daisies, narcissi, honesty, roses and forget-me-not. However, also included in the range were a number of more unusual designs which featured butterflies, peacock feathers, fish, seaweed, boats, trees and landscape. The toadstool design was probably also a Florian pattern when first produced late in 1902, and did not acquire its Liberty Claremont name and style until 1904. The designs cover the surface, reflecting the influence of William Morris and the Arts and Crafts Movement, and flowing naturally over the curves of the pot. Grounds were usually pale, with

patterns often drawn either in complementary colours or in darker shades of the ground colour, for example blue on blue or green on green. A copy of an order from a Montreal retailer, dating from 1902 or 1903, lists the following Florian colour versions: blue and yellow, green, blue and yellow, lilac and purple, blue, and gold and blue. Other colours were also made, for example salmon and green. These colours paved the way for the green and gold Florian design 404017, and its pink ground derivative which was known as Alhambra. This version, although tube-lined in Moorcroft's department, was decorated in on-glaze enamels elsewhere in the factory, and so was not signed. Factory records show that the Alhambra name was not entirely fanciful, for the ware was sold in Madrid. In the early 1900s Moorcroft began to replace the coloured grounds with white and cream, and at the same time the designs became simpler but more colourful. These changes were made possibly by better colour control during the firing, and by the availability of new colours developed by Moorcroft himself.

From about 1904 Moorcroft began to move away from Florian, which he regarded as a specific range. However, Macintyre's continued to use the name as a generic term for all the art pottery made in his department, and for this reason it remained in regular use among retailers and in the press; the *Pottery Gazette* was still referring to Moorcroft's pottery as Florian Ware in 1913, while a list of stock taken from Macintyre's to the new factory at Cobridge, and dated 27 October 1913, mentions brown Florian. The Florian backstamp remained in use until about 1905, when it was replaced by the ordinary Macintyre printed mark. Florian Ware was also known by other names, mostly those chosen by particular retailers, the only exception being the short-lived Butterfly Ware, introduced in 1899 and notable for its Florian-like butterflies in gold on a dark ground, and its own printed backstamp. Among the retailers' names were Burslem Ware, used by Liberty to describe a number of non-floral designs, Hazledene for the green tree or landscape design and Claremont for the toadstool design, both used by Liberty, and Hesperian Ware, used by Osler's. A letter from E Watling of Osler, addressed to Mr Moorcroft and dated 15 April 1902, described how the Hesperian name evolved:

'How does Hispalian strike you? (taken from the name of an old Persian city) Or Hesparian – from the Garden of the Hesperides. Then there are such names as Amarantine, Auranian, Calabrian, Castalian etc. Considering the eastern origin of so many of your forms I incline towards a name that is suggestive of the Orient & think that perhaps Hispalian would not be a bad one. It is easy for the tongue and memory. Please let me know what you think. A friend here more strongly inclines towards Hesperian as being more phonetic.'

These individual versions of Florian often carried backstamps incorporating the retailer's name.

Moorcroft devoted almost as much of his time to the design and making of tableware as to his ornamental pieces. Some carried Florian patterns and was designed, decorated and signed in exactly the same way as the vases made in his department. However, he was also responsible for the Dura and Aurelian tablewares that were advertised regularly in the *Pottery Gazette*. Dura Ware, although not signed, was produced in his department, and designed and decorated in the same way as the Florian Ware. The Aurelian tableware, with its printed and enamelled decoration, although designed by Moorcroft, was produced in another part of the factory, together with the Aurelian vases that continued in production after he took over the art pottery departments. The original Tinted Faience and the 'Household Requisites', as Macintyre's called them, were still made, but his responsibility for these was vicarious if it existed at all. A catalogue, published in 1902, provides a record of what was being produced at that time. Five pages of designs are devoted to the Dura Ware, and credited to Moorcroft, four to Aurelian Ware, and four to Tinted Faience and miscellaneous articles, only some of which were designed by Moorcroft. The tableware that bore the

12 Thrower Harry Bailey, with his assistant Mrs Farrington, photographed in 1930

13 The Moorcroft decorating shop in 1933, from The Pottery Gazette

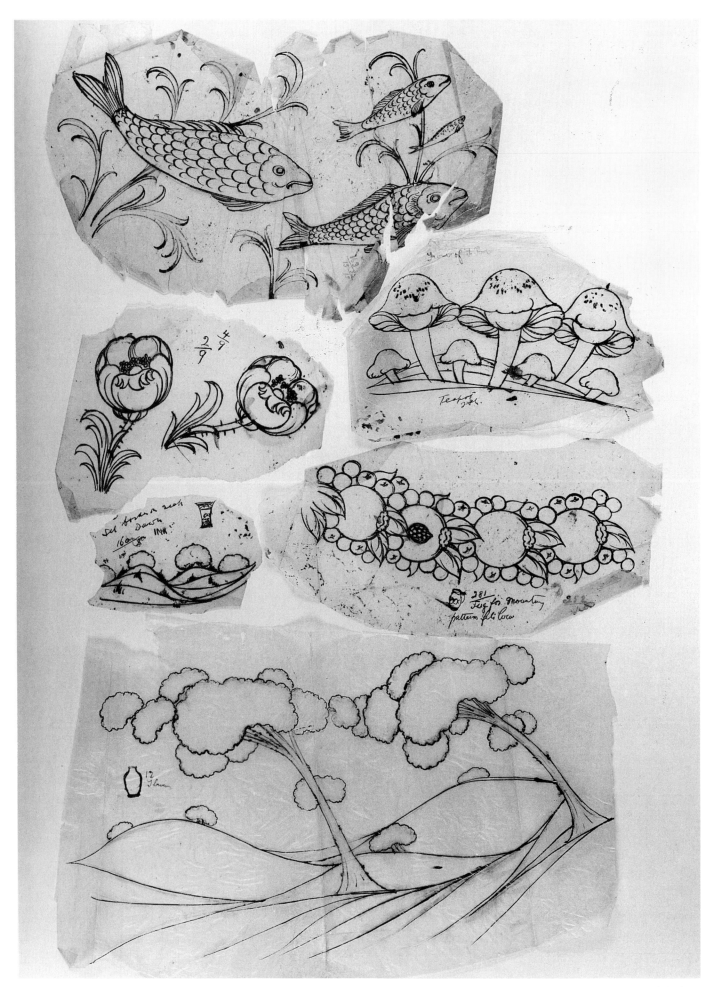

14 Preserved at the factory are many drawings by Moorcroft used for transferring the designs onto the ware. Moorcroft would adapt each design to fit a particular shape, using a purple ink on tracing paper. The decorators would then rest the paper against the green (unfired) ware and rub on the design, leaving a pale outline to be followed by the slip-trailers. Exactly the same system is still used today

14a Drawings by Moorcroft, for the '5 o'clock tray' with below an example of the tray, made for Liberty's in c 1908, length 15¼ ins. Presumably made as a tea tray, perhaps with matching tableware

Gesso Faience backstamp, with its design outlined in white, is represented by a jug and cruet set, showing that some of this early range was still in production in 1902. Also present are some surprising mismarriages, for example Moorcroft Florian-type decoration on revived rococo shapes. Tableware was an important part of Macintyre's production throughout this period and as late as 1905 new teapot and jug shapes designed by Moorcroft were being registered. At the same time, extensive ranges of Florian tablewares were produced, featuring the same patterns and styles as the ornamental wares, and often carrying Moorcroft's signature. Many of these were bought by metal manufacturers and silversmiths in Sheffield and Birmingham for mounting or setting into silver and electro-plated stands, while others were supplied in bulk to American retailers, such as G. J. Bassett of New York.

Moorcroft enjoyed great freedom at the Washington Works, and indeed his work during this period established his own reputation rather than his employer's. He made full use of Macintyre's London showrooms, at 4 Thavies Inn, Holborn Circus, EC4 and was able to exhibit his work widely. He was also able to establish good relationships with a number of retailers, at home and abroad. A letter written by Francis T Meyer, an American importer, and dated 24 October 1902, comments on this: 'Your new ware we found prominently shown and highly spoken of at Liberty's.'

A few years later, in October 1907, a friend writing to William from New York described a display at Tiffany's: 'I am just coming again from Tiffany building, where I saw your lustrous new ware. I think it is very fine indeed! All has a label, that shows who is the artist, who responsible for it. No mentioning the firm's name at all. Lucky man you are! They stand in a fine place, on a special table . . .' The same writer then goes on to compare the Moorcroft display with others in the store of Doulton's new flambé and W Howson Taylor's high fired Ruskin pottery. The international success achieved by the Moorcroft rather than the Macintyre name may well, in the long term, have influenced Macintyre's in their decision to give up the making of ornamental pottery, but in the short term they appear to have been well pleased, and were happy to bask in the reflected glory when Moorcroft won his first gold medal at the St Louis International Exhibition of 1904. It is often forgotten that Henry Watkin, Moorcroft's Managing Director, also won a gold medal at St Louis, for the development of an oven heat recorder. The friendly relationships between employer and employee is underlined by a letter written in November 1904 to Moorcroft by Corbett Woodall Macintyre's Chairman: 'I am buying quite a lot of your vases – half a dozen this week . . .' Success brought orders from many directions. In 1906 there were sales to Australia, Germany and Canada, while Rouard of Paris were sending 'big orders' for vases which they then converted into lamps. The following year Marshall, Field of Chicago were notable among North American buyers. Other awards followed St Louis, with Moorcroft winning another gold medal at Brussels in 1910 and a Diploma of Honour at Ghent in 1913. Moorcroft was also becoming well known locally, with over 25 of his wares being shown in a Modern English Pottery exhibition at Manchester City Art Gallery in 1909, along with work by Pilkington's, Bernard Moore and Howson Taylor, and his developing reputation may have inspired Charlotte Rhead's father to write to him in December 1906 asking if he would employ her and her sister Dolly as tube-liners. In the event, nothing came of the idea. Inevitably, success brought problems. Demand outstripped production, and it was the small retailers who suffered. R J Russell of Sidmouth, Devon, wrote to complain in November 1909: 'Dear Sir, Can you send us along *at once* (so that we can show them for Xmas) the Pottery bought last Feb, which you *promised* for Easter & again for August but same did not arrive. *Do please* send along now & oblige. Yours truly . . .'

From 1904 onwards Moorcroft began to introduce a range of new designs that moved steadily further away from Florian. The first of these was probably the monochrome Flamminian Ware, whose oriental simplicity was far removed from either William Morris or Art Nouveau. At the time of its introduction, Moorcroft wrote a description of this new ware: 'Flamminian Ware is so called owing to its entire effect being due to the action of flame. It is only at a certain temperature that the bright luminous Red is obtained. The fire plays upon the body its own, and leaves its expression in thousands of forms as the waves leave the sand on the sea shore. The forms of Flamminian Ware, like historical types of an earlier period, are always expressive of the material'. The roundels which decorate Flamminian were registered in April 1905, and a letter from Liberty, dated 19 May 1905, shows how quickly the ware went into production: '. . . we herewith give you a list of articles, samples of which we wish you to make in the New Red Ware.' Copy invoices issued later the same year indicate some of the shapes being made in Flamminian: Red – candlesticks, children's mugs, sardines and stands, square fruit trays, plaques, pots and pedestals, oblong bowls; Green – inkstands, pentrays, sardines and stands, pots and pedestals, square fruit trays, bowls, candlesticks, trinket box, honey box, early morning set, covered cup and stand, covered muffin, dessert plates, sugar and cream. Another new introduction was Ruby Lustre, a rich red lustre laid over Hazledene, Claremont and other patterns. First made in 1907, it is this that Moorcroft's friend saw on his visit to Tiffany's and described in the letter quoted above. Although they were not high fired flambés in any way, these ruby lustres were obviously seen by retailers as directly competitive with the flambés of Doulton or Howson Taylor, with some preferring them without the underlying decoration. This is clearly indicated by a letter dated 10 August 1908 from Christian Dierckx, at that time acting as Macintyre's agent in New York: 'Referring to the red decor, I would kindly request you to get me up say half a dozen pieces, good shapes, in a *plain*, solid deep red color, without the decorations as in the Tiffany, and also if possible half a dozen in a handsome green, leaving the choice of the color to your good taste. The special merit would have to be in the quality and shade of color, as well as in the gracefulness of the shape.'

These ruby wares may have been Moorcroft's first use of lustre but others soon followed, for some of the simplified floral patterns on pale grounds had begun to appear with pale yellowish lustre overlay during 1907. Indeed, Moorcroft appears to have been interested in lustre effects at quite an early date for among the factory papers is a copy of a catalogue of liquid golds and lustre colours made by Poulenc Brothers of Paris, and printed in Newcastle, Staffordshire in January 1898. Three lustres are marked, lustre black No.1, lustre blue chatoyant no.1, and lustre red chatoyant no.1. Copy invoices dated 1909 mention yellow lustre ginger boxes, as well as additional items in the Flamminian range, including pot pourri jars, clockframes, ginger boxes, fern pots, miniatures and a variety of tablewares.

The period 1905 to 1911 seems to have been a particularly creative one for Moorcroft, with a number of new decorative patterns appearing. Some had a simplicity, delicacy and elegance that linked them with contemporary textile and interior design trends, while others were richer and more robust. Among the former were a number of simplified Florian designs, used on white or cream grounds enriched with heavy gilding, as well as several new designs. The first of these was probably Eighteenth Century, with its swags of English flowers draped carefully and rather formally round the ware to capture the spirit of the contemporary Adam revival, and in production at least by May 1906, when it appears in an order from the T. Eaton Company of Canada. The same order mentions Cream Medallion, while subsequent orders from various retailers refer to White Adams pattern, White Florian, Florian XVIII Century and XVIII Century Florian with Gold Finish. Related in style were the Berry, Tudor Rose and Bara patterns, the last-named exclusive to Liberty in the home market, and inspired probably by Liberty fabrics of the same period. Among the more robust patterns were the rich versions of the Claremont or toadstool design, in both red and green colourings, the dark green trees or landscape design, and a range of new

15 A display of Moorcroft Ware photographed at the British Industries Fair in London in 1918

16 The Moorcroft stand at the British Industries Fair, White City, London, in 1926

patterns which included Florian iris and new cornflower, introduced by 1910, the new brown Florian mentioned in a letter from Osler's dated December 1909, and the Spanish design, developed in 1910. Also related to these new floral designs were pansy, made with yellow, white and green grounds from about 1910 and wisteria. These richer patterns culminated in the pomegranate design, in production at least by April 1911 when the New York agent, Christian Dierckx, refers to it in a letter, and made in both red and green versions.

With these patterns Moorcroft entered a new era. His style of drawing became bolder, sweeping over the surface and thrown into relief by the increasing use of dark and mottled grounds. The far more delicate style of slip trailing allowed the colours to spread beyond their defined areas and to merge together to add texture and tonal effects, many of which were deliberately accidental. Some retailers did not appreciate these changes. One, writing from Huddersfield in 1906, commented: 'We agree with you that a certain amount of atmospheric effect is very pleasing and we do not expect a hard line between the colours, but when the colour has run as badly as it has on many of the pieces, we do not think that anyone can appreciate them, and we do not care to offer them for sale.'

However, in general reactions were favourable. In 1913, *The Connoisseur* reviewed an exhibition of Moorcroft ware at the Royal Institution, Albemarle Street, London with great enthusiasm: 'The examples shown included various specimens of types already familiar, but each susceptible to infinite variety of expression. The pieces . . . are wrought in simple but beautiful forms and decorated with appropriate designs. These show a marked originality of treatment, more especially as regards the colouring, which is never glaring or obtrusive . . . some of the most beautiful effects which have been produced in modern ceramic art were obtained.' Another area of activity that expanded considerably after 1905 was the supply of decorated ware for mounting or setting into plated stands. In 1913 Moorcroft calculated that selling to electro platers accounted for about one sixth of his annual turnover, but it is important to remember that he had virtually no control over the metal mounts or stands at this time. A letter from J H Potter, a manufacturing silversmith in Sheffield, written in November 1906, is a typical example of this kind of business: 'Will you kindly make us a sardine dish, plain, something after the style of the enclosed sketch. Any mould of a similar kind will do so that we can mount it up on a stand – we will provide a plated lid – in a pattern to match the jam jar we had from you. Also can you let us have half round or similar shaped Cheese Dish Cover, also Sugar Basin and Cream Jug suitable for mounting into sugar and cream frame, all to match.' Many similar letters and orders from platers and silversmiths have survived, including ones from Baum Brothers, James Gallimore and George Traws of Sheffield, and Evans & Matthews, Green & Cadbury and Walsham & Co of Birmingham.

However, by far the most important development of the 1900s was the close relationship between Moorcroft and Liberty's. Florian and other wares had been advertised regularly in Liberty catalogues such as their Yule-Tide Gifts from the early 1900s, and Liberty's had their own printed backstamp from about 1903. This was used extensively on the Flamminian and other ranges associated particularly with the Regent Street store, such as Hazledene and Claremont, Tudor Rose and Bara, names that were probably created by Liberty's themselves. Murena was another Liberty name, given to the pomegranate design, but rarely used. Liberty's also commissioned Moorcroft to produce a range of commemorative wares, the first of which was a mug made for the coronation of Edward VII in 1902, designed by Lasenby Liberty and made expressly for Mr & Mrs Liberty. Other commissions followed, including a coronation mug for George V in 1911 and a peace mug in 1919, while the order for production of the 1911 mug decorated with Lord Norton's patriotic Coronation Song also came through Liberty's.

It is clear that Liberty's were probably Moorcroft's most important client during the 1900s, but the relationship was more than just a commercial one. A friendship developed between Moorcroft and Alwyn Lasenby, Lasenby Liberty's cousin and a partner in the company and this was to prove of vital importance in the years to come. A letter from Alwyn Lasenby, dated 4 January 1903, shows that the friendship had already been established for some time: 'I think the specimen vase of Toadstool design is a very charming piece, and a very happy addition to my collection.' Another letter, written in July 1905, compliments Moorcroft on his recent successes: 'I think it splendid how well you have been doing this year, when on all sides I hear how badly others have. We are also "holding our own" in L & Co.'

It is equally clear that the relationship was between Liberty's and Moorcroft, not Macintyre. Even though Liberty never used the Moorcroft name in their catalogues until after 1913, all the correspondence was always addressed directly to Moorcroft, and it was this personal element that was to prove vital in the light of subsequent events. Despite the fact that it was Moorcroft's name that was becoming well known around the world, Macintyre's do not seem to have been unhappy, and the relationship between the two appears to have been amicable, at least until 1911. In that year the first signs of a rift appeared, in a serious disagreement between Moorcroft and his Managing Director Henry Watkin about the costs of the art pottery department. From this moment on, Watkin and Moorcroft rarely saw eye to eye. In addition, Macintyre's were in any case reconsidering the whole future of their ornamental and tableware departments, with a view to concentrating on the production of electrical porcelain. In the event, the decision was not made until that latter part of 1912, and Moorcroft appears to have been formally told that his department was to close in a letter from Corbett Woodall written on 10 October. A subsequent letter, written by Woodall on 21 November, confirmed the details:

'At a meeting of the Directors today it was resolved that your department should be continued until the end of the Company's financial year which is the 30th of June.'

17 Display of Dawn landscape wares at the 1926 British Industries Fair

18 Persian Ware, illustrated in the Pottery Gazette in July 1916

19 Advertisement from Liberty's Yule-Tide Gifts catalogue, 1919, showing Claremont, pomegranate and orchid designs

20 Advertisement from Liberty's Yule-Tide Gifts catalogue, 1916 showing a range of powder blue wares with rose panels

21 Liberty's Tudor Tearooms in about 1920, equipped with Moorcroft Powder Blue tablewares

I hope that within that time it will be quite convenient for you to make arrangements so that you have no idle period on your hands.'

Moorcroft began immediately to plan a new factory where he could continue to produce the ware that he had made so characteristically his own. His first scheme seems to have been for a company that would take over Macintyre's decorative pottery production, using Macintyre staff and equipment, in new premises, but still using the Macintyre name. A document written by Moorcroft outlines the structure of such a company, and is headed: 'Formation of a Company for making Decorated Pottery to trade under a name such as "James Macintyre 1912 Ltd"' The difficulties inherent in such a scheme must have quickly become apparent, for in early December Moorcroft received from Reginald T Longden, a local architect with practices in Stoke and Leek, outline plans for a complete new factory. At the same time, negotiations were started between Longden, Moorcroft and Sneyd Collieries, owners of a plot of land at Cobridge. By 13 January 1913 an option on this land had been secured and the architect had drawn up a complete set of plans.

The pace of events makes it clear that Moorcroft had found a source of finance for setting up his new business, for he was in no position to build a new factory from his own resources. He had considerable investments in shares, notably in the Canadian Pacific Railway, which at that time was paying good dividends, but these in themselves were clearly inadequate to cover the expenditure needed. In December 1912 he had calculated that the sum required to build a new factory, set up in business and operate for three months was £8000. To find this sum he turned to Liberty's, probably through the good offices of his friend Alwyn Lasenby, and discussions took place early in December. On 14 December, he was able to write to Lasenby with some optimism:

'I am extremely hopeful the result will be wholly satisfactory. We have a production entirely our own & a staff personally trained during the last 15 years & workers never more efficient than now. I would deeply appreciate to learn of your general approval. The present company made me a very valuable gift by their decision to discontinue making every form of decorative pottery.'

Negotiations then continued between Moorcroft and the Liberty directors, with Harold Blackmore playing an important role. Blackmore, related to the Liberty family by marriage, was their legal adviser as well as a director, and was to act for many years as Moorcroft's company secretary. On 23 December Liberty's agreed in principle to financing half the cost of the new venture, subject to various conditions being met. Moorcroft appears to have then written to Corbett Woodall, informing him of this decision, for on 2 January 1913 Woodall wrote and thanked him, adding: 'I had an interesting conversation with Liberty's and have given them the best possible account of yourself . . .' A few days later there was a meeting between Liberty's and Watkin and Woodall, the result of which was a complete change of direction on Liberty's part. They wrote to Moorcroft to withdraw from the scheme, which they now believed to be financially unviable. They had also become aware of the uneasy relationship that existed between Moorcroft and Macintyre, adding:

'We have, rightly or wrongly, formed the opinion that when you actually come to break off with Macintyres, a good many obstacles will be put in the way of the transaction going through smoothly . . . and it is partly on this account we have decided to stand out.'

Moorcroft set to work at once to repair the damage. The architect drew up new plans for a smaller and much cheaper factory, to be built for a total of £2020, the setting up and operating costs were reconsidered, and a new total cost estimate of £3000 was sent to Liberty's. At the same time, as though to make amends for the difficulties Macintyre's had caused. Corbett Woodall wrote to Moorcroft to say that: 'If it is of service to you you are quite at liberty to tell Messrs Liberty & Co that the Directors of James Macintyre & Co will put no obstacle in the transfer of the Florian

Department. Since you have been with us the Department has been entirely under your control . . .' A search started for a new site, and Moorcroft considered a number of possibilities, including land in Burslem owned by John Heath, an existing factory at Fenton, the property of Ernest Bilton, and some land in Cobridge, owned by the Sandbach School Foundation, a charitable trust, and tenanted by a brick and tile company. In the event , it was this site that Moorcroft favoured, and he wrote to Harold Blackmore accordingly; '. . . the site is an excellent one. It is opposite a public park & adjoins the station & railway & is on the main road . . .' Negotiations for the purchase of 5930 square yards at the price of 2/– per square yard were started, a lengthy process due to the trust status of the owner. Moorcroft also sent Liberty's an estimate for the first year's turnover, a total of £7000 made up as follows: China dealers £3500, Electro-platers £1500, Furnishing Houses £1000, Jewellers & Co &1000. At the same time, he drew up a list of his major clients at home and abroad. The international list included major retailers in Paris, Madrid, Brussels, New York, Boston and New Zealand, while the principal clients in England, listed in order of importance, were Liberty & Co, F & C Osler, Shoolbred & Co, Army & Navy Coop Society, Civil Service Stores, Derry & Toms, Jones & Higgins, Townsend & Co of Newcastle and Stonier & Co of Liverpool.

On 12 February Liberty's wrote to Moorcroft to say that they were prepared to accept the revised scheme, and enclosed a formal proposal. The basis of this was that Liberty's would put up two-thirds of the cost, and Moorcroft one third, with much of Liberty's share being in the form of a Debenture loan secured by a first charge on all the assets. Two types of shares were issued, with Liberty buying a block of A shares, and Moorcroft the B shares, both of which had a value of £1. Moorcroft had more shares, but Liberty's investment was the greater, because of their £1800 debenture loan. In addition, Moorcroft was to give his services to the company for life, while the agreement was to be for ten years in the first instance. The two directors were to be Alwyn Lasenby and Moorcroft. The next day Moorcroft wrote to Liberty's to say that he had agreed 'entirely to all you suggest'. The pattern thus established gave Liberty's control of the new company, and this was to be maintained until 1947.

In early May the purchase of the land was finalised, at a final cost of £534 4s 8d and on 15 May the architect returned the contract signed by the builder, Joseph Cooke of Porthill, who had estimated £1400 for the job, and agreed to complete the building in ten weeks. Liberty's were able to persuade Macintyre's to extend by one month, until 31 July, the period of notice to be given to Moorcroft and the staff of his department, to enable them to move straight into a completed building. Work on the building started in late May, and progressed rapidly, with regular stage payments of £250 being made to Cooke from the new company's account at the National Provincial Bank at Burslem. At this critical point in his career, Moorcroft was able to enjoy the support not only of his friends at Liberty's but also of his new wife, Florence Lovibond, who he had married early in 1913 prior to moving into a new house in Trentham. Florence was an unusual woman, by profession an inspector of factories for the Home Office, and she had a considerable influence on the design of the new factory. It was in many ways a revolutionary building. The site itself was high and open, with good views, and the factory buildings filled under a third of the available space. Moorcroft's experiences at the Washington Works, a large conventional multi-storey Victorian pot bank ranged round a central courtyard, had made him determined to overcome the dangers and difficulties inherent in such a structure. He wanted to avoid the continual carrying of heavy materials and wares up and down stairs, the problems posed by dust and glazes, and the dangers of inserting machinery into spaces not designed for it. As a result he chose a small single storey layout, with well defined working areas, plenty of light and adequate lavatory and washing facilities. Cast iron frame construction and plain windowless exterior walls certainly simplified construction, but the speed of the operation was still

22 Liberty leaflet of about 1920, showing the Powder Blue tableware range

remarkable. It was the first truly modern factory building in the Potteries and the first to provide one floor production. At the same time, its modern functionalism also reflected the fact that it was the cheapest building the architect could provide, while complying with the requirements of the new Pottery Regulations made under the Factories Act, which had also come into effect in 1913. The Moorcroft factory, simple and elegant in its own way, was an interesting blend of avant garde functionalism with the studio philosophy of William Morris and the Arts & Crafts Movement. The building was enlarged in 1915 and then again in 1919–1920, with Liberty's writing in February 1919 to approve the estimated building costs of £490, but the design principles and style of the original structure were carefully maintained, and so even today the revolutionary qualities of the factory can still be appreciated. In 1985 a fully detailed report and description of the factory was published by the Stoke-on-Trent Historic Buildings Survey of the City Museum and Art Gallery, entitled *Moorcrofts Pottery Factory Drawing No B199*.

Building work was largely completed by the end of August and Moorcroft was able to move into the new factory the plant and equipment that he had acquired from Macintyre's and other sources. He also moved in his small team of craftsmen and women, about 34 people, many of whom had worked with him at the Washington Works. Apart from the many lady decorators, the key people were Henry Barlow, the foreman turner, John Thomas Tudor, fireman and placer, William H Barlow, mould-maker, jollier and presser, and James Newman the thrower, all of whom had been with him since 1897. Another thrower, F W Hollis had also worked at Macintyre's before he joined Moorcroft in 1916.

However, by this time Moorcroft's relationship with his former employers had, as anticipated by Liberty's deteriorated to such an extent that on August 13 he received a letter from Macintyre's solicitor barring him from entering the Washington Works. There were a number of causes for this state of affairs, but the primary one seems to have been an interview with Moorcroft published in the March 1913 issue of the *Pottery Gazette* to which Henry Watkin took great exception. In June Moorcroft made himself even more unpopular by complaining when all the employees in his department received their formal notice to quit, and then there was a long and accrimonious dispute about the value of some moulds that Moorcroft wished to purchase from Macintyre's. This dragged on into 1914 before it was finally resolved. Despite these difficulties Liberty's and Macintyre's were able to agree on 24 June on the wording of a circular letter that was sent out to the press, stockists and suppliers in early July, printed on the new Moorcroft stationary, and explaining the background to the new company. Once the inevitable teething troubles were over, production got under way, and the new company settled into a pattern not radically different from that which had prevailed at the Washington Works. The new oven was soon being fired, initially with the patterns developed at Macintyre's, and at the first Annual General Meeting held on 8 October 1914, the directors were able to report a trading profit of £49 15s 8d. There is some inevitable confusion about the wares being made during this transitional period. Some carry only signatures, some carry the new impressed marks adopted at Cobridge, while some have the printed Liberty marks used until 1913. There are also many wares with dates for the latter months of 1913 and early 1914; it is natural to assume that these represent early Cobridge production. During this time Moorcroft was also coming to terms with all the demands associated with running a business, the regular Board meetings, the annual stocktaking, cash flow, and the claims made by suppliers, rating authorities and the inland revenue. Liberty's were very supportive during this difficult learning period, and the principle was quickly established whereby Moorcroft sent them a weekly demand, including his salary, which they paid promptly by cheque. In August 1915 there was a second issue of debenture shares, to cover a further loan from Liberty's of £1200, secured by a second charge on the factory and assets.

During the negotiations with Liberty's there had been discussion of the need to produce some cheaper or simpler lines that would serve as bread and butter production for the new factory. A range of printed wares were considered, but in the end it was the Powder Blue tableware range that was the most important introduction during the early days at Cobridge. First produced in 1913, the range was originally known as Blue Porcelain by Moorcroft as he used a porcellaneous body similar to that developed by Macintyre's for their electrical wares. In any case, power blue had a different meaning in commercial terms, and was used to describe blue-ground ornamental porcelains made by Wedgwood, Royal Worcester and many other factories. It was Liberty who named the range Powder Blue, but Moorcroft sold it as Blue Porcelain. It also became generally known as Moorcroft Blue. This speckled blue tableware was an immediate success, giving Moorcroft the steady production runs the new factory needed. It was made in an enormous variety of shapes and sizes, the majority of which were thrown and hand-finished on the lathe, yet the prices were reasonable. For example, in the early 1920s a 29 piece breakfast set cost £2 10 3d and a 1½ pint teapot 4/6d. Powder Blue tableware was used by Liberty in their new Tudor Tea Rooms and the range was also well regarded by contemporary critics. In 1922, for example, a writer in the *Daily Mail* commented: 'Nothing, for instance, would give one a greater sense of satisfaction at breakfast time than a set of cups and saucers in the deep lapis lazuli blue of some of the Moorcroft pottery . . . apart from whole sets, there are many smaller pieces that may give brilliance and originality to the morning mealtime table.' In 1937 Nikolaus Pevsner included the tableware of his *Enquiry into Industrial Art in England* and wrote: 'One of the best contemporary sets, William Moorcroft's famous Plain Blue, was designed in 1913, and is, in spite of that as "modern" as anything created now, and as modern as Josiah Wedgwood's sets, i.e. undatedly perfect.'

Blue Porcelain remained in production until 1963, and over the years various other colours were tried out, none of which were particularly successful. During the 1930s, for example, the following tableware colours were recorded on copy invoices: jade green, sunray, green, orange, old gold, celadon, pink, biege and brown, matt green, yellow (not the same as sunray), honey, green and silver, cobalt and chrome, matt blue. In addition, Blue Porcelain itself was made in a variety of shades, including blue, dark blue, light blue and special pale blue, partly as a result of natural variation in the firing, and partly because various retailers actually specified that the blue should be light or dark. '. . . must be dark blue. The customer has returned those sent previously as too light' is typical of a number of comments about the colour of Blue Porcelain recorded in the factory order book of the mid 1930s.

New patterns were also developed as quickly as possible, including late Florian, Persian and the range of designs based on fruit and flower panels contained in reserves. Of these, Persian with its rich colours and Middle Eastern flavour was the most distinctive, drawing together ideas taken from both Isnik pottery and carpets. A letter from Moorcroft to Alwyn Lasenby, written in January 1913, underlines the link with carpets as a source of inspiration: 'I have in course of development the scheme you suggested of fish and seaweed, also an idea of developing a decoration with a red background echoing the spirit & the movement of an oriental carpet.' These new patterns were in production by 1915, for a notebook in Moorcroft's hand, dated 21 July 1915, lists the following patterns in production: green Flamminian, Pansy, Pansy celadon, cornflower, Spanish, Claremont, Hazledene, pomegranate, blue and white panel, Persian, wisteria, toadstool, tree, Red Persian, 2170. This list also makes it clear that there was a tree pattern quite separate from Hazledene, and that toadstool and Claremont were not the same. Earlier copy invoices also refer to another mushroom design, called Fungus. Decorative designs were also introduced and were based on the Blue Porcelain slip, with the addition of trailed patterns, lustre effects and colour variations. New shapes also appeared, for example a water bottle with cover, ordered by Mappin & Webb in February 1914.

The outbreak of the First World War had little initial impact on the factory, but the introduction of conscription in 1916 reduced the workforce. However, production was maintained and export business was expanded in line with government requirements. Along with many other potters, Moorcroft also took on government supply contracts, making beer and shaving mugs, hospital inhalers and other basic domestic wares for the army. In the latter years of the war this became an increasingly important and lucrative part of the business. For example, in one three month period from July to September 1917 income from War Office contracts totalled £307 2s 3d; during a similar, but slightly longer period, income from Liberty's, Moorcroft's largest client came to £207 0s 11d. When the war ended in 1918, production returned to normal, and Moorcroft launched a policy of expansion. A government Return of Employees of 1918 lists 32 women and 15 men, including Moorcroft, who refers to himself as 'Potter, Chemist, Designer, Managing Director, Secretary'. Early in 1919, he advertised in the *Sentinel* for 'young lady freehand paintresses' in order to increase output. The same year the factory was enlarged. Also in 1919 Moorcroft took part in the War Memorials Exhibition at the Victoria & Albert Museum, following a particular request to do so from the Museum's Director, Cecil

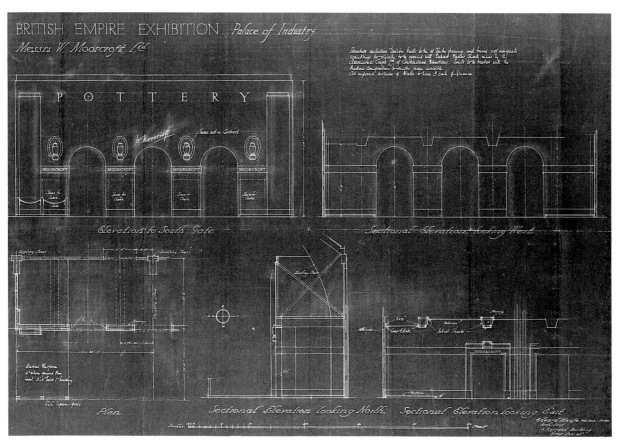

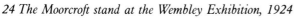

23 Edward Maufe's design for the Moorcroft stand at the 1924 British Empire Exhibition

24 The Moorcroft stand at the Wembley Exhibition, 1924

25 Display of 1930s wares, as illustrated in The Pottery Gazette

Harcourt-Smith, showing an earthenware vase and a pair of mugs.

The relationship with Liberty continued to flourish, due largely to the success of the business. On 11 September 1919 Alwyn Lasenby wrote to Moorcroft: 'We enclose a copy of the Balance Sheet and Profit and Loss Account. They make a very satisfactory showing, and of course are even better than they look. The position is undoubtedly a very sound one, and you are again to be congratulated on the year's trading.' Another letter, written by Lasenby a few months later, in March 1920, shows that he was far more than just a sleeping partner:

'I am very pleased with the progress I saw & am full of hope for the future development. Have you yet had time to get the plan of the ground with existing buildings got out for me? Will you mark each building, what it is used for when you get it? I am anxious about the better facilities for drawing the ovens, sorting and despatching of orders. To help the growth of trade you must have this seen to; then providing you can get the necessary help to leave you more time for the creation & production and selling, I believe you will soon find you are in a better position to execute the many orders that now have to be held back.' Indeed, the many letters that survive from this period reveal just how dominant the Liberty influence was. All cheques, including Moorcroft's salary and commission payments had to be countersigned in London. For example, a letter from Liberty dated 4 February 1925 says:

'I enclose herewith your Salary cheque due to 31st January 1925 £125.0.0 and your commission cheque for January sales £43.5.10.'

To put these in context, the weekly costs for running the factory,

are also revealed in a letter from Liberty's, dated 28 August 1919: 'Wages & sundries £106.13.3 Coal (Sneyd Colleries) £58.10.8 Harrison (clay and pottery supplies) £43.0.0'

It is clear that throughout this period Liberty's were, in both financial and practical terms, the controlling partner, as well as the largest client. At the same time, it was a relationship that benefited both sides. Profits climbed steadily, reaching a peak of £7895 14s 5½d in 1923. By 1921 all the Debenture loans had been repaid by Moorcroft, but Liberty's retained control by converting the first loan of £1800 into extra B shares, thus maintaining the two-thirds, one-third split. New Liberty nominee directors were appointed in 1921, with William Sheet and John Llewellyn joining the Board. In 1936 they were replaced by William Dorell and Captain Ivor Stewart-Liberty. Throughout the 1920s and into the 1930s the company continued to trade successfully, although losses were recorded in 1928 and 1931, and both dividends and bonuses to shareholders were paid regularly during this period. Without any major financial worries, Moorcroft was able to concentrate on design and production, and it was during the 1920s that he really developed his international reputation. Rich colours, strongly drawn patterns and a range of naturally-inspired subjects, some old, some new, characterise the wares of this period. English flowers were still used, in new and more vibrant combinations, but more powerful were the patterns based on fruit, toadstools, and exotic flowers. The landscape design reappeared in new forms to reflect the tastes of the time, the sombre, nocturnal Moonlit Blue, the dynamic colours of Eventide or Autumn Tree as it was known in the factory and later, the cool tones of Dawn, with its matt finish. Other designs reappeared

26 Page from a catalogue of pewter-mounted Tudric Ware, made by Haseler's initially for Liberty's, and subsequently sold to other retailers

27 Page from a giftware catalogue issued by the retailers Connell of Cheapside, showing Tudric pewter-mounted Moorcroft pottery

constantly over a long period of time, including peacock feathers, fish, and butterflies. Animals never featured, except on some commemorative wares. As with the Florian Wares, the relationship between the surface pattern and the shape of the pot was always carefully controlled. It is difficult to find a Moorcroft piece with unhappy proportions, a feature that reveals his debt to the Far East. Some shapes he used throughout his life, others appeared once only.

A copy invoice dated March 1923 reveals some of the range of patterns in production: pomegranate, poppy, moonlit blue tree, wisteria, heartsease, orchid, cornflower, toadstool, seaweed, green, lemon, old gold and mauve lustre, blue porcelain, King's Blue, as well as rouge flambé and stoneware. Apparently the names heartsease and pansy were used fairly indiscriminately to describe similar designs. Others mention anemone, in production by 1919, pansy and narcissus. Export business was flourishing, particularly in Canada, Australia and other colonial markets, but there were also important sales to South America, Scandinavia and elsewhere. The developing reputation of Moorcroft himself was underlined by a comment on an order from Buenos Aires, typical of many in similar style: 'Selection left to Mr Moorcroft's good judgement'. He was also enjoying a friendship with Cecil Harcourt Smith, the Director of the Victoria & Albert Museum, who wrote to him in October 1924:

'I want to write and thank you very much indeed for the china you have sent . . . I cant tell you how nice it is & how much we enjoy looking at it. I can assure you everyone who sees it admires it tremendously.'

Another area of expansion was the production of wares made to be mounted in silver, electroplate, pewter and brass. While sales of conventional ornamental and tablewares to electro platers still provided an important part of the turnover, Moorcroft began increasingly to produce wares that were designed to be mounted. Ashtrays and other wares with brass and nickel mounts were exhibited in 1920 by W Hutton of Birmingham, and the previous year Moorcroft had started to commission mounts from the Duchess of Sunderland's Cripples Guild. The best of these were made by Francis Arthur Edwardes, a family friend and a teacher at the Burslem School of Art who Moorcroft continued to patronise after his departure from the Duchess of Sutherland's Guild in 1920. Edwardes, a traditional silversmith in the Arts and Crafts style, made a number of highly decorative silver and silver on copper mounts during the 1920s and 1930s. In 1923 a vase with oxidised silver mounts was included, with other Moorcroft wares, in an Exhibition of Industrial Art of Today, at the Victoria & Albert Museum. More significant in commercial terms was the association with W Haseler, for whom a wide range of wares in at least six patterns were made for mounting in hammered pewter. Many of these were made for Liberty's and carried the impressed Tudric Mark but it is important to remember that Tudric was not an exclusive Liberty range and was also sold by Haseler's to other retailers. A letter from Haseler's, written in January 1926, also requests that a range of Blue Porcelain teawares be supplied, for mounting in pewter. Also popular throughout this period were the little plaques and medallions made to be mounted as brooches. These were made in a variety of patterns, and with interesting

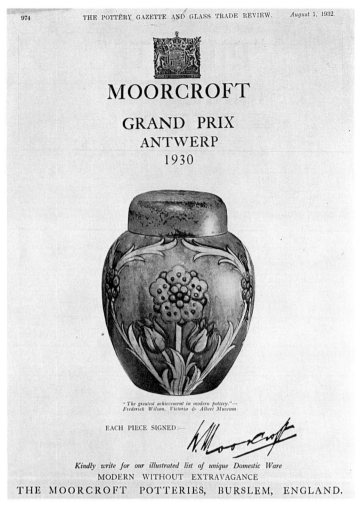

974 THE POTTERY GAZETTE AND GLASS TRADE REVIEW. *August 1, 1932*.

MOORCROFT

GRAND PRIX
ANTWERP
1930

"The greatest achievement in modern pottery."—
Frederick Wilson, Victoria & Albert Museum.

EACH PIECE SIGNED:—

Kindly write for our illustrated list of unique Domestic Ware
MODERN WITHOUT EXTRAVAGANCE
THE MOORCROFT POTTERIES, BURSLEM, ENGLAND.

28 Moorcroft advertisement from a series published in The Pottery Gazette and other journals during the 1930s

29 Moorcroft advertisement from The Pottery and Glass Record, April 1937, showing coronation wares and an early limited edition

THE POTTERY AND GLASS RECORD

MOORCROFT
(REGISTERED)
POTTERY

EACH PIECE IS DESIGNED
& SIGNED BY:—

Potter to Her
Majesty the Queen

THE MOORCROFT POTTERIES. BURSLEM

coloured glaze effects. A letter written in 1917 refers to plaques and medallions with the 'pansy design & special glaze colouring' priced at between 60s and 72s per gross, assorted colours. Medallions were also made in smaller sizes for mounting in rings and pendants.

The greatest achievement of the 1920s were the monochrome glazed wares, which reflected Moorcroft's increasing interest in purer and more directly oriental forms of ceramics. Lustre glazes continued in use at least until the early 1930s, in monochrome colours, often in conjunction with the speckled Blue Porcelain slip, and as an overglaze on decorative patterns. For a short period during the early 1920s dark monochrome stonewares were also made. However, it was the high temperature flambé glazes that were to represent Moorcroft's highest achievement in this field. Like many of his contemporaries, for example C. J. Noke, Bernard Moore and Howson Taylor, Moorcroft had always been interested in transmutation glaze effects. He had experimented with high temperature firing at the Washington Works, but he was not able to develop the process fully until he built himself a special flambé kiln at Cobridge in 1919. In this oven he was able to unlock the secrets of the process that was to turn him into a Master Potter during the 1920s and 1930s. The tones of deep red chartreuse and purple that characterise Moorcroft flambé are endlessly varied. Unlike Noke and Moore, who attempted to produce a controlled sang de boeuf colour, Moorcroft revelled in the unpredictability of the firing, the eccentricity of the colours and the uniqueness of each piece that was produced by this barely controllable process. He was always secretive about the flambé firings, and insisted on controlling the oven himself during the long days and nights.

Flambé exists in two main forms, first as an eternally varied glaze effect fired over a conventional decorative design, and second as a pure glaze effect in its own right, the latter related to Chinese monochrome and high temperature porcelains of the 17th century. It was this that Moorcroft considered his greatest achievement, a view underlined by the admiration of pure flambés attracted from scholars and connoisseurs all over the world. A factory order book of the mid 1930s reveals the international popularity of the flambé wares, and the many different styles and colours produced. Among the patterns recorded in this book with flambé are autumn leaf, leaf, toadstool, fish, Persian and waratah, while the descriptions of the pure flambés are even more varied and include rouge, rouge with yellow, peach bloom, sang de boeuf, plain, mauve and dark.

The success enjoyed by the flambés was in part due to Moorcroft's regular displays at exhibitions and trade fairs. The company first showed at the British Industries Fair in 1915, and this annual event then became an important part of the Moorcroft calendar. For some years the displays were funded by, and organised in close cooperation with Liberty's, and the Liberty studio designed the distinctive stand that was to become a memorable feature of each year's Fair. More important, however, for Moorcroft's international reputation, was the company's display at the British Empire Exhibition held at Wembley in 1924. By August 1923 a large space in the Pottery and Glass Section of the Palace of Industry had been reserved and a few weeks later the architect Edward Maufe had prepared designs for the exhibition stand. This, an elegant scheme in a restrained version of contemporary classicism, was to be one of the most distinctive features of this part of the exhibition. Indeed, the particular character of this section, organised by Lawrence Weaver, was established by the stands of the three major exhibitors, Wedgwood, Pilkington and Moorcroft. Inside the stand, the ware was displayed in natural oak cabinets, designed and made by Liberty's. These cabinets were subsequently reused at the annual British Industries Fairs, and are now incorporated into the Moorcroft Museum at the Moorcroft factory. Their original cost was £684 4s 9d. As with other trade shows, Liberty's were involved in all stages of the planning and organisation of the Wembley display. In addition to buying all the ware on display, Liberty's also insisted on a notice on the stand directing retail purchasers to their Regent Street

30 *Selection of medals awarded to William Moorcroft. Top row, left to right: British Empire Exhibition, Wembley, 1924; Royal Warrant Holders Association, dated 28 March 1928; St Louis Exhibition, 1904; National Medal for Success in Art awarded by the Department of Science and Art in 1899. Bottom row, left to right: Antwerp Exhibition, 1930; Ghent Exhibition, 1913; Brussels Exhibition, 1910*

31 *Diploma commemorating the Grand Prix awarded to Moorcroft at the Antwerp International Exhibition of 1930*

store, and so were in effect acting as Moorcroft's London showroom.

The Wembley exhibition was a success for Moorcroft, both in terms of trade and as a means of international promotion. Press coverage was extensive and favourable. The *Furnishing Trades Organiser* wrote: 'The famous Moorcroft ware is exhibited in a handsome and distinguished environment' while the correspondent for *World's Work* was particularly impressed by the colours: 'The Wembley exhibit of Moorcroft pottery is an assembly of many colours, but not a single one is out of place. Nothing harsh or crude obtains; all are beautifully blended. Some of the contrasts are a delight to dwell upon.' An even more glowing report appeared in the *Daily Graphic* on 28 June 1924, under the heading A Potter of Genius: 'Such a master potter is William Moorcroft, an artist of the most distinguished gifts . . . The master of today is the old master of tomorrow, and the discerning collector does not lose sight of this fact. Moorcroft pottery will be the quest of collectors of future generations, for it is the perfect expression of the potter's art . . . In design, harmony, delicacy and richness of colouring this stands unique among ceramic ware of today. Baron Hayashi, the Japanese Ambassador, in purchasing two Flambé vases last year, said the Moorcroft vases were in every way the equal of early Chinese work – a very great compliment indeed.' The *Graphic* then went on to describe some of the exhibits, notably vases decorated with Moonlit Tree and Autumn Tree designs and some of the flambé effects, in particular a beaker '. . . of a rich opal, flecked with golden, feathery cloudlets, and melting into purple and russet towards the base. It is the work of a poet.'

Moorcroft's success was not confined to Britain, for his display at the Exposition des Arts Decoratifs in Paris in 1925 was also well received. At Antwerp in 1930 he won a Grand Prix, and at Milan in 1933 a Diploma of Honour. However, it was the Wembley display above all that confirmed Moorcroft's popularity with Queen Mary and other members of the Royal Family.

Moorcroft's Royal associations started in 1913, when Queen Mary admired some examples of Florian Ware during a visit to the Potteries. The same year the Queen bought some pieces from Harrods, and Moorcroft was quick to write to the store to find out exactly what she had chosen. His letter, dated 13 May 1913, goes on to explain that, as he was soon to take over the production of all Macintyre's decorative pottery at his own works, 'Such information regarding the Queen's purchases would help me . . .' Queen Mary was, in any case, a regular visitor to the British Industries Fair, and she soon developed the habit of visiting the Moorcroft stand, which she continued to do every year until the outbreak of the Second World War. In 1916, for example, *The Court Journal* was able to report:

'Another exhibit of great interest is that of Messrs W Moorcroft Ltd . . . Mr Moorcroft's designs are, of course, known the wide world over, and Her Majesty graciously acknowledged this on her visit.' Subsequent Royal visits were reported with ever-increasing enthusiasm. In 1917, the *Journal* wrote: 'On the occasion of the Queen's first visit Her Majesty honoured Messrs Moorcroft by inspecting their exhibits . . . the Queen purchased two specimens of the pottery,' and the following year: 'Queen Mary purchased a vase decorated with orchids on a special texture glaze, and it is not surprising that Her Majesty's keen perception selected this treasure of the collection.' The *Journal*'s report for 1920 stated: 'Her Majesty the Queen, who is an expert in these matters, immediately noticed a beautiful vase which, curiously enough, was the first of its kind to be manufactured, and purchased the same . . . the upper portion is a rare dove colour and the lower part like the colour of a raven's wing. There is drawn on the vase a border of ornament in grey-green, yellow and purple . . . His Majesty the King was keen in his admiration of a group of blue porcelain.'

Royal support continued through the 1920s, with quite a close

32 Family group at Trentham in 1930, taken after Florence Moorcroft's death. Left to right: Edith Parry (Florence's sister), her husband Philip Lestor Parry, William Moorcroft, Walter Moorcroft, Beatrice Moorcroft

33 William and Hazel Moorcroft (née Lasenby) on their wedding day, in October 1928

relationship developing between Moorcroft and Queen Mary. 'The Queen has a rare taste for form and colour' Moorcroft told a reporter from the *Daily Sketch* in October 1931, and then went on to say that her favourite colours were blues and greens. The previous year the *Daily News and Westminster Gazette* carried on its front page a long letter by Moorcroft, written in connection with the opening of the Wedgwood Bicentenary Celebrations by Princess Mary, and illustrated by a Moorcroft vase presented to the Queen. The prominent publication of this letter, which extolled the virtues of natural inspiration and handcraft techniques for the potter, was probably a reflection of Moorcroft's receipt of a Royal Warrant in 1928. His appointment as Potter to Her Majesty Queen Mary was a particularly personal honour, and John Bemrose, writing in 1946, drew a parallel between this and other Royal appointments such as the Master of the King's Music, and described it as 'the laureate of a noble profession'.

From about 1930 the phrase Potter to Her Majesty the Queen was widely used on labels, in advertisements and as an impressed backstamp. Royal visits to the British Industries Fairs continued through the 1930s. The *Pottery Gazette*, reporting one such visit in 1932, commented: 'Her Majesty the Queen, inspecting some of Mr Moorcroft's work under a magnifying glass, frankly admired its charm.'

In February 1935 the Queen, the Princess Royal and the Duke of York all purchased rouge flambé bowls, and the Queen a matching cigarette box. At the same time the Duchess of York bought a teaset decorated with the leaf and berry pattern on celadon. This Royal purchase was widely reported, and later the same year the Hudson's Bay Company ordered identical rouge flambé wares for branches in Edmonton, Vancouver, Winnipeg, Victoria and Calgary, requesting that the wares be accompanied by 'showcards stating that the pieces were as purchased by the Queen'. Moorcroft pottery continued to attract Royal interest until William's death in 1945, and then Queen Mary transferred her affections, and the Royal Warrant, to his son Walter, telling him when she met him at the British Industries Fair in 1947 that she was sorry her old friend had died and wishing him every success.

The 1930s saw another dramatic change of style for Moorcroft, with a return to pale grounds and the extensive use of matt glazes. Designs were simplified to suit current tastes and the patterns became more abstract. Some earlier designs were redrawn in the new styles, for example honesty, toadstool, peacock feathers and fish, while other new ones, such as yacht and waving corn, both developed from original ideas by Moorcroft's daughter Beatrice, were introduced. Semi abstract and Art Deco style borders were also widely used. Moorcroft responded to current enthusiasms for handmade pottery by emphasising the handcraft qualities inherent in his wares, and by relying increasingly on simple forms and pale colours. These changes were noted by the *Pottery & Glass Record* in 1932: 'There were several Moorcroft flower holders of a quite new shape, finished with texture glazes and with the hand work of the thrower visible on them.' In November the same year the *Sphere* published a dramatic photograph of a fine example of what Moorcroft referred to as his 'natural pottery'. At the same time, wares with coloured patterns and flambé glazes were still being produced and sold alongside the pastel tones and matt glazes the market demanded. It was a difficult period for Moorcroft who, like most British potters, had suffered directly the effects of the Wall Street crash of 1929. Major clients had disappeared overnight, markets had shrunk, and decorative pottery seemed out of place in a depressed world. Export sales were now more than ever the lifeblood of the business, with Moorcroft forced to depend more and more on his reputation in the international marketplace. In 1934 and 1935, for example, his biggest market was Canada, followed by Australia and New Zealand, but sales were also made to retailers in the United States, Bermuda, Mexico, Argentina, Holland, Norway, Italy, Spain, Sweden, South Africa, Rhodesia, Kenya, Egypt and Japan. The export markets still favoured the traditional colourful patterns,

and the most popular during this period were heartsease, wisteria, pomegranate, windswept corn, weeping beech, pansy, leaf flambé and waratah. Each country inevitably had its own special requirements. The Japanese, for example, liked the pottery to be as individual as possible.

In 1934 the Japanese Ambassador returned some leaf flambé plates to the factory, requesting they be replaced by ones with a deeper tone, while an order from Tokyo for plaques, bowls and vases specified that 'each must be different in shape, size, pattern, colour, price etc. colour something like an oil painting'. In November 1937 Moorcroft wrote to *The Times*, drawing attention to a letter he had received form the Director of the Deutsches Museum, Munich, which thanked him warmly for his gift of some 'outstandingly beautiful pieces . . . that will form a centrepiece of our ceramic exhibits'. The same year Moorcroft's display at the Paris Exposition Internationale des Arts et des Techniques was enthusiastically acclaimed in *La Revue Moderne des Arts et de la Vie*: 'le plus célèbre artist céramiste d'Angleterre a dù rechercher un cadre vaste pour y présenter un ensemble d'oeuvres qui fut digne de son magnifique talent. Moorcroft a brillamment moissonné les plus hautes récompenses, consécrations d'un art qu'il a porté à son apogée. Les plus illustres collectionneurs du monde entier, les critiques formés par toutes les cultures ont rendu hommage à la valeur exceptionnelle de ses créations.'

In the home market it was a matter of survival, and this was achieved by the expedient of producing an extraordinarily diverse range of wares. Pieces were sometimes made to match the colour of fabric samples supplied by retailers, or in individual styles or colour schemes. Named children's mugs were advertised in 1935, and produced some response. One retailer requested '24 mugs with names (most popular names) such as Peter, John, Michael, Ann, Mary, Elizabeth, Joan.' Haseler's, and other silversmiths and platers continued to order wares for mounting, and the factory sales record book for 1935 includes references to a silver cover costing £20, and a gold mounted vase priced at £7 10s. Motto wares and lustre were still being made, as well as an extensive range of lamps, in both coloured designs and 'natural pottery' and supplied with or without shades. Unusual shapes still in production in 1935 included a bacon dish, three and five bar toastracks, lotion bottles (for Austin Reed), a square meat plate and an octogonal oatmeal, honey and marmalade jars, cocoa jugs and egg stands, as well as jugs and inhalers for the War Office. Most table and domestic wares were made in plain colours, but patterns were also used and among the designs recorded most frequently are heartsease, pomegranate, yacht, feather, vine, pansy, autumn leaves, leaf flambé and waratah. However, it is the astonishing range of patterns being made in 1934 and 1935 that reveal just how flexible the factory had to be to survive. Recorded in the factory sales book for those years are the following: autumn leaf, leaf, maple leaf, panel leaf, leaf columbia, leaf and vine, leaf and berry, fruit and foliage, blue leaves and red cherries: toadstool, mushroom: grass, harvest grass, June grass, wheat, waving corn (or windswept corn), trellis and wheat panels: trees, Eventide, Moonlit blue, weeping beech, weeping willow: feather, peacock, vine and feather, panel feather: yacht, fish, bird: pomegranate, vine, acorn, red mulberries, blackberry: wisteria, pansy, pansy large flower, heartsease, chrysanthemum, cornflower, honeysuckle, poppy, waratah, Tudor rose, heather, tulip, lotus flower, lattice flower: Persian, powder, Queen's Jade, medieval, sundawn, eternity, Royal Academy. Many of these were being made in numerous colours, and in both matt saltglazed and conventional clear glazed finishes. Feather, for example, is recorded in the book in cream, orange, green, dull green, parchment, celadon and orange, sepia, ivory, green and blue, mottle and saltglaze, yacht in celadon, gold, broken green, ivory, white, chestnut, sunray, cream, parchment, green and blue, orange and old gold, tree in green, pink and jade, and black, toadstool in orange, ivory, chestnut and saltglaze, and wheat in yellow, brown and cream and green. Some familiar patterns were also being made in unexpected colours, for example blue pansy and blue pomegranate.

Some of these patterns, such as medieval or eternity are completely unfamiliar today, and they may simply have been unusual versions of conventional patterns, perhaps made for particular retailers. Eternity may have been used to describe a particular shape of bowl with motto and roses decoration. Easier to explain is Royal Academy, for in 1935 Moorcroft took part in the *Exhibition of British Art in Industry*, held at the Royal Academy in Burlington House between January and March of that year, and planned to encourage public support for modern design in contemporary industry. It is not possible to establish from the exhibition catalogue exactly what Moorcroft showed, but clearly there was at least one pattern or colour version produced specially for the display, for the factory sales book includes several orders from retailers requiring 'replicas of the pottery on show at the Academy'. Interestingly, Liberty's did not take part in the exhibition, although other retailers, such as Heal's and Harrod's, were represented.

The diversity of production during the latter part of the 1930s is also reflected by the list of patterns displayed at the British Industries Fair in 1939, many of which were shown in a number of colours as well as the flambé and saltglaze finishes: orchid, spring flowers, South African lily, anemone, leaf, autumn leaves, bluebell wood, windswept corn, natural, orange blossom, flaming June, cornflower, waratah, love in a mist, blue and white, lilium auratum, pomegranate, heartsease and Moonlit Blue.

During the Second World War, this pattern was maintained. Exports of decorative pottery, helped by government contracts, enabled Moorcroft to retain his workshops and a skeleton staff. For the home market, he rose to the challenge posed by government restrictions on the manufacture of decorative pottery by designing a range of plain ivory Austerity tableware, his contribution to the official price-controlled utility scheme. On 18 September 1942 *The Times* published a letter from Moorcroft, expressing the hope that standards of design could actually be improved by the government restrictions: 'Form exquisitely balanced, pure in tone and texture, is as refreshing as early morning in the country with the song of bird. But the maker of pottery alone can eliminate the fault in shape that so easily destroys beauty and truth. If the order for simplicity which the Board of Trade has been compelled to enforce can lead to this high ideal then a great advance will have been made through the influence of adversity.' The letter was accompanied by an Austerity tea service, which *The Times* described in favourable terms: 'The service seems very practical . . . it has a comely look, almost amounting to elegance, and it shows how pleasing a well-planned simplicity can be.' There were other indications that Moorcroft still enjoyed a considerable reputation, for example an article by Sir Cecil Harcourt Smith, now retired from his position as Director of the Victoria & Albert Museum, published in the *Spectator* on 15 January 1943, which said, in the context of post-war design: 'In Moorcroft, we possess an artist-potter whose wares are upholding the supremacy of British production both at home and overseas.' However, the war years were really a time of desperate struggle for Moorcroft, with only his will power keeping the factory, and himself, alive.

In 1945 he was taken ill, and his son Walter came home from the army on compassionate leave. A few days later, on October 14, William Moorcroft died. Walter, demobilised without returning to

active service, took over the running of the factory.

Right up to his death, William Moorcroft was an autocrat in his own world. He insisted on total responsibility for every aspect of production, from the design through to the sale and distribution of the wares. He never employed a manager, or any other designer. Yet, at the same time, he fully appreciated the skills of the craftsmen and women that he employed. Designs were adopted, abandoned and then re-adopted for no particular reason. Half-completed pots would suddenly interest him no more, and be relegated to the ever growing pile beneath the work bench. Customers were expected to tolerate the unpredictabilities of the firing, and still pay good prices for good pieces. Alternatively they might be given the pots for nothing. Yet beneath all this was a sound business sense and a dedication that kept the pottery open when all around were closing down. He was inclined to refer to himself as an industrialist and, in an age when art pottery had come to be an anchronism, he was an important bridge between commercial production and the studio potter. He was, above all, a master potter and in 1913 he described his feelings towards his chosen field: 'I have always been charmed with the sense of freedom and individuality that has characterised the work of the Eastern potter, and it was after long dreaming of what was possible in this direction that I was first able to express my own feeling in clay. Perhaps no other material is so responsive to the spirit of the worker as is the clay of the potter, and my efforts, and those of my assistants, are directed to an endeavour to produce beautiful forms on the thrower's wheel, and added ornamentation of which is applied by hand upon the moist clay. This I feel imparts to the pottery the spirit and the art of the worker, and spontaneously gives the pieces all the individual charm and beauty that is possible, a result never attained by mechanical means.'

The reputation that Moorcroft enjoyed ensured he had plenty of imitators. Some companies actually produced wares designed to be mistaken for Moorcroft pottery, using the same patterns and colours. In the 1920s a Staffordshire company produced copies of Moorcroft pomegranate wares, using the same colours and the same slip-trailed technique. These wares are unmarked, but occur on shapes Moorcroft never used. The Bough Pottery in Edinburgh also produced Moorcroft replicas, and Jacobs produced a Moorcroft biscuit tin. Other companies did not actually reproduce Moorcroft designs but copied techniques and colours to create a generally similar style. The early success of Florian Ware probably encouraged Minton to launch their Secessionist Ware in 1902, a range of slip-trailed ornamental and domestic wares designed by John Wadsworth and Leon Solon. Solon had, in any case, been producing slip-trailed tiles and panels since the 1890s. Another early imitator was George Cartlidge, whose Morris Ware, designed for S. Hancock & Company during the early 1900s, was decorated with slip-trailed floral patterns with a strong Florian bias. Jacobean Ware produced during the 1920s under the Royal Stanley label was a transfer-printed design of fruit and flowers in typical Moorcroft colours, while Hancock's Rubens Ware of the same period featured a painted pomegranate design. It was inevitable that slip-trailing should achieve a general popularity during the first decades of this century, particularly among tile designers and manufacturers, and so it would be unjust to call an artist such as Charlotte Rhead an imitator of Moorcroft. Yet Moorcroft has to take the credit for introducing a style of decoration that was to be so influential among both art and commercial potters.

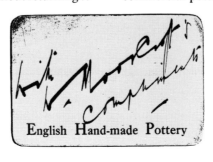

English Hand-made Pottery

Thomas Moorcroft 1849-1885

1 Selected pieces from a bone china tea service, made by E.J.D. Bodley with floral decoration in raised gold, from designs by Thomas Moorcroft. Each piece in the set features an individual design. Notable also for its stork handles in contemporary Japanese style, the service was registered in April 1875.

2 Watercolour by Thomas Moorcroft of orchids, probably drawn at Trentham by permission of the Duke of Sutherland. For this painting Moorcroft received a Silver Medal in 1875, awarded in the Department of Art and Science's national competition. For an orchid vase by William Moorcroft based on his father's watercolour, see page 88.

1

2

William Moorcroft at James Macintyre & Company, 1897-1913

Macintyre Art Pottery, 1894-1898

Macintyre's opened an Art Pottery department in their Washington Works in the early 1890s. Little is known about their earliest productions, except that, from the start, designers drawn from outside the factory seem to have been involved. Two early ranges, Taluf Ware and Washington Faience, were shown at the *Exhibition of Decorative and Artistic Pottery* held at the Imperial Institute in 1894. Both featured slip decoration, both had printed backstamps, and some Washington Faience designs were registered. The sprigged ornaments on Washington Faience were modelled by Mr Wildig.

In 1895 Harry Barnard was appointed director of the art pottery department. Trained in slip decoration at Doulton's Lambeth studio, Barnard introduced a new style of ornament featuring Art Nouveau patterns built up by hand in raised slip. This was named Gesso Faience and the range was launched in 1896–1897 with its own printed backstamp. In 1897 Barnard left Macintyre to join Wedgwood, where he continued the development of slip decoration.

When William Moorcroft took over the design and production of the art pottery in 1898, he had been working for Macintyre's for nearly a year. During this time he had designed new shapes for both useful and ornamental ware and introduced the Aurelian Ware that was decorated in printed patterns with enamel and gold. By the autumn of 1897 his new domestic ware had progressed far enough for the firm to register some of his new shapes, in November 1897 and January 1898, and three Aurelian Ware designs were registered in February 1898. The process of slip-trailing was by this time used widely and Moorcroft had begun experimenting with it for the decoration of the plain slipware before the end of 1897. During this experimental period some printed Aurelian designs were combined with slip-trailing.

1

2

3

4

1 Early Macintyre art pottery, c1894. Left, Washington Faience jug with sprigged decoration modelled by Wilding; right, Taluf Ware jug with carved slip decoration in typical Macintyre colours. Faience jug height 5¹/₂ ins

2 Gesso Faience with slip-trailed decoration probably designed by Harry Barnard, c1896. Large jug height 7¹/₂ ins

3 Gesso Faience vase, with design of English flowers in raised slip, probably by Harry Barnard, c1896. Height 13 ins

4 Group of wares decorated with raised slip designs by Harry Barnard at Wedgwood, c1898

5 Macintyre shape teapot, registered in 1897, with Gesso Faience mark, but with cornflower design by Moorcroft. Both the colour and the style suggest that this was an early example of Moorcroft slip decoration. Height 6½ ins

6 Vase with Moorcroft Florian decoration and additional gilding, c1898. Height 10¾ ins

7 Group of Aurelian Ware with transfer-printed patterns enriched with red enamel and gilding, designed by Moorcroft in 1897. Largest vase height 10 ins

8 Group of wares showing Moorcroft's development of his design from the printed Aurelian Ware vase on the left to the blue Florian Ware on the right, via slip-trailed tablewares, c1897. Jug height 6½ ins

Florian Ware, 1898-c1906

Florian Ware, the range that established Moorcroft as a designer, was launched in 1898. Decorated with flowing floral patterns in applied raised slip, a distinctive technique and style that Moorcroft was to use for the rest of his life, Florian Ware represented a blend between contemporary Art Nouveau and the decorative traditions of William Morris and the Arts and Crafts Movement.

There are many different Florian patterns, the majority based on English flowers. Poppies, violets, tulips, iris, forget-me-nots, cornflowers, daisies, roses, narcissi, honesty were all used, as well as peacock feathers, butterflies, fish and the first of the landscape designs. At first coloured grounds were used, pale blues and greens often with patterns in darker tones of the same colour, but later white and cream grounds became more common, decorated with patterns in pinks, yellows and brown. Some designs, particularly those on white grounds, were enriched with gilding. Between September 1898 and September 1902 about ten Florian designs were registered, one of the last being the landscape design. The shapes were designed by Moorcroft as well as the patterns, and the coordination between the two is characteristically good. Shapes were inspired first by Middle and Far Eastern ceramics and later, from about 1900, by classical pottery. Florian Ware was marked with a printed backstamp, and it was the first range to be regularly signed or initialled by Moorcroft. The backstamp remained in use until about 1905. Some versions of Florian Ware carried different backstamps, for example the Hesperian Ware made for Osler's, and the rare Butterfly Ware.

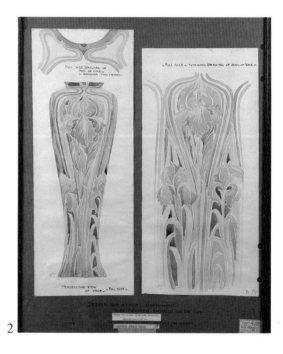

2

1

1 Three early Florian Ware vases decorated with the iris pattern in typical colours. The green vase is dated March 1899, and the blue vase carries the Hesperian Ware backstamp.
Largest vase height 16½ins
2 Design for a vase by William Moorcroft for which he received a bronze medal in 1898 in the annual National Competition organised by the Department of Science and Art.
3 Group of Florian Ware decorated with versions of the iris design. The four on the left show the early version of the pattern; the white ground version on the right is c1900.
Largest vase height 12ins
4 Group of Florian Ware decorated with versions of the violet design, which was registered in September 1898. All 1898-c1900. The smallest vase also carries a Liberty mark.
Largest vase height 12½ins

3

4

2

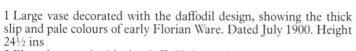

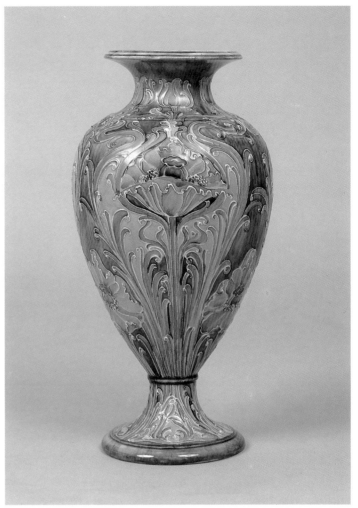

1 Large vase decorated with the daffodil design, showing the thick slip and pale colours of early Florian Ware. Dated July 1900. Height 24½ ins

2 Plate decorated with the daffodil design in typical Florian blues, c1900. Diameter 12½ ins

3 Florian vase decorated with the poppy design, registered in September 1898. Height 12¾ ins

4 Group of Florian Ware decorated with the poppy design, showing some of the early colours. The dish and the blue and yellow vase also carry Liberty marks. All c1900. Largest vase 12½ ins

3

4

1 Two Florian vases decorated with versions of the peacock design, registered in October 1899. This is probably Moorcroft's most characteristic vase form, and it is still used today. Both c1900. Larger vase height 14½ ins

2 Florian vase decorated with the peacock design in unusual colours, c1900. Height 10¾ ins

3 Group of Florian Ware decorated with versions of the peacock design in typical early colours, all c1900-1902. Largest vase height 11 ins

4 Group of Florian Ware decorated with the cornflower design, all c1900-1902. Largest vase height 13½ ins
5 Group of Florian Ware decorated with the daisy design, showing the development of the pale grounds. The vase on the right carries the Hesperian Ware mark, and has the typical mauve colour. All c1902. Largest vase height 10 ins

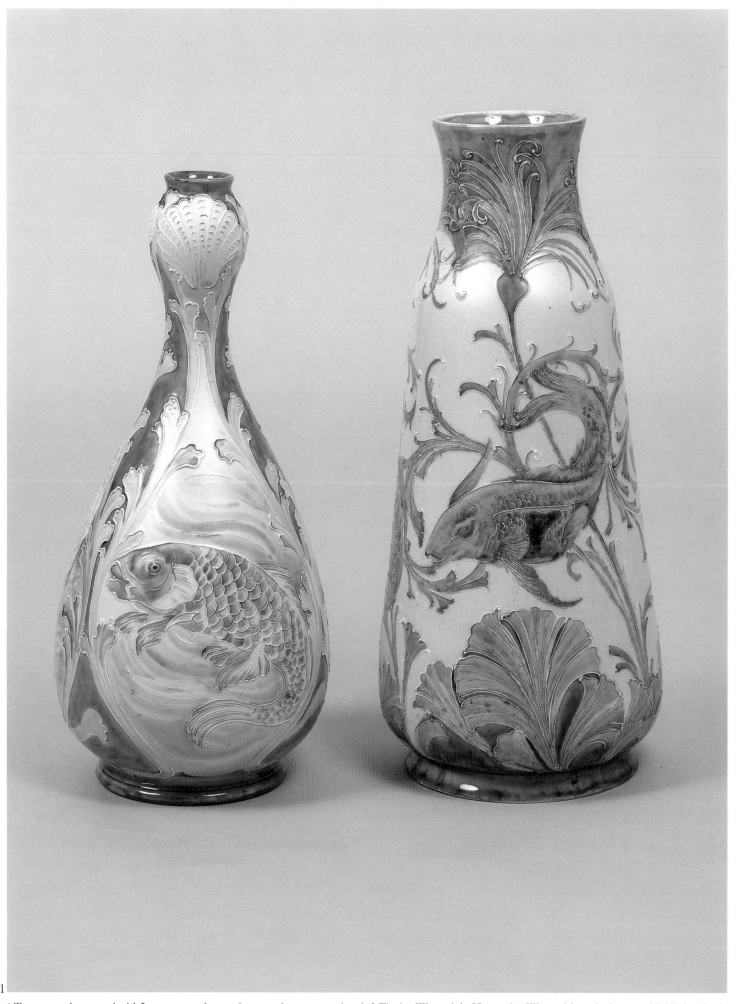

1

1 Two vases decorated with Japanese-style carp in an underwater setting, left Florian Ware, right Hesperian Ware with typical mauve highlights, both c1902. Larger vase height 13 ins

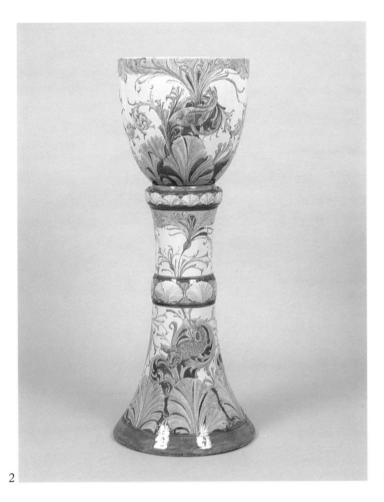

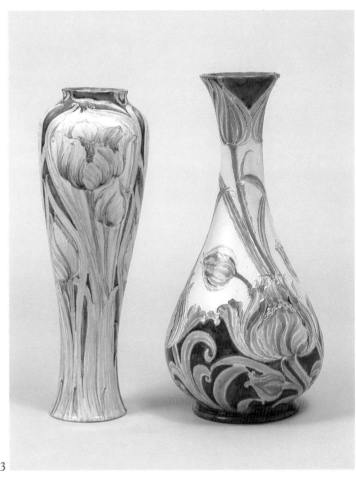

2

3

2 Hesperian Ware jardinière and stand, decorated with carp, seaweed and bands of shells, c1902. Overall height 34½ ins
3 Florian Ware vases, decorated with versions of the tulip design, c1900. Larger vase height 16½ ins
4 Group of Florian Ware decorated with the tulip design, and Hesperian Ware vase second from right, all c1900-1902. Largest vase height 13½ ins

4

1

1 Group of Florian Ware decorated with the lilac design, c1902. Largest vase height 12 ins
2 Group showing different versions of the lilac design. Left, two Florian vases c1902, right, three pieces showing the pale grounds and rich gilding of the post-Florian period, c1905. Largest vase height 8 ins
3 Two Florian Ware vases decorated with the honesty design, showing the characteristic roughened and matt finished surface, c1903. Larger vase height 11ins

2

4 Jardinière decorated with daisy and poppy designs, additionally enriched with silvering, c1904. The shape is one that Moorcroft adapted from classical pottery, excavated at Pompeii. Made for Shreve & Company, San Francisco. Height 8¼ ins

5 Group of vases with butterfly designs, left to right, small vase with unusual colours and lustrous finish, marked Watkins Leadless Glaze, c1904, Butterfly Ware vase with characteristic dark ground, rich gilding and printed backstamp, design registered in 1899, Florian Ware vase registered in September 1898, and Florian Ware vase c1900. Largest vase height 11 ins

1

1 Group of Florian Ware decorated with tulip, poppy, wild rose and other flower designs, showing varied styles of slip trailing, c1899. Largest vase height 9 ins

2 Group of Florian Ware decorated with tulip, forget-me-not and other flower designs, most of which were registered in 1898, c1899. Largest vase height 9½ ins

2

3

3 Group of Florian Ware decorated with primrose, crocus, fresia, tulip and other flower designs, c1899. Largest vase height 11 ins

4 Group of Florian Ware decorated with the iris and cornflower designs showing the distinctive salmon and green colours, c1900. Largest vase height 16 ins

4

1 Group of wares decorated with Florian-style designs in blue and green, 1902–1911. The two candlesticks and the bowl with handles carry Liberty marks. Larger candlestick height 9¾ ins
2 Group of Florian Ware decorated with assorted flower designs in blue, green and yellow, c1902. The dish has a Liberty mark and is in typical Liberty colours. Largest vase height 8½ ins

3

3 Group of wares decorated in Florian style with poppies, tulips and roses. The green ground vases have Liberty marks and the largest vase has a poppy design registered in September 1902. All c1902–1903, except the brown Florian vase with handles which is c1909. Largest vase height 12 ins

4 Group of Florian and similar ware decorated with various fresia, poppy, cornflower and harebell designs, c1902–1904. The smallest vase has a Liberty mark. Largest vase height 9½ ins

4

1

2

1 Group including tazze and plates from a dessert service and a Liberty bowl, all decorated with Florian-style designs, c1902. Vase height 8 ins

2 Group of four Florian Ware vases, two decorated with seaweed designs related to the Lorne shape Dura Ware jug on the left. The jug shape was registered by Macintyre's in 1897. All c1902. Largest vase height 8 ins

3 Group of wares with Florian-style designs of poppies, daffodils and other flowers in characteristic Liberty colours, c1902. the small vase should have a flared rim. Largest vase height 9½ ins

3

Later Macintyre Wares, 1902-1913

Although the styles and techniques of Florian Ware remained in use, Moorcroft began to move in new directions from 1903. Green and Gold Florian, design 404017, registered in January 1903, marked this change of direction. Intricately drawn and often richly gilded, the design with its tendril-like leaves has a strong Art Nouveau feeling. The main design features a flower and a tulip bud, but there is also a variant, a stylised dahlia flower, which has the same registration number.

There are three colour ways. The green is the most common and shows the best use of the gilding, the pink is less common and the blue is rare. These wares usually carry a printed Macintyre mark, the registration number and a Moorcroft signature. However, as a rule the pink version is unsigned, as these were finished outside Moorcroft's supervision in the enamelling rooms. This range was probably in production until about 1908. The other great change was the move to white or cream grounds, made possible by an increased range of colours and better firing control. The first of these was probably the Florian poppy design, 401753, registered in September 1902, and developed from the Dura tableware range. It was still being produced to order as late as 1914. This trend culminated in the Eighteenth Century Pattern, in production

from 1906 to about 1914, and the related designs introduced between 1907 and 1909. These featured roses, forget-me-nots and other garden flowers either contained in panels or drawn in sprays or garlands that made the most of the pale grounds.

5

4 Vase decorated with the standard Green and Gold Florian design in green, with typical rich gilding, c1903. Height 16½ ins

5 Goblets decorated with the dahlia variant of the Green and Gold design, c1903. The pink version in unsigned. Larger goblet height 9½ ins

4

1

1 Group of vases decorated with the Green and Gold Florian design in green, c1903. Largest vase height 10½ ins
2 Group of vases decorated with the Green and Gold Florian design in blue, c1903. The vase without gilding is also unsigned, and so may simply be unfinished. Largest vase height 11 ins

2

3

3 Group of wares decorated with the Alhambra version of the Green and Gold Florian design in pink, c1903. All unsigned except the slender vase second from the left. Largest vase height 12 ins
4 Group of wares decorated with a rose garland design on a white ground, enriched with gilding, c1907. Vase height 12 ins

4

1 Group of wares decorated with a poppy design, showing the three colour ways. Registered in September 1902, the design is closely related to one of the Dura tableware patterns. Largest vase height 7 ins
2 Group of wares decorated with the poppy design, 401753, all c1903–1904. The shaker with its threaded base is unusual and is an enlargement of the miniature salts and peppers in the form of bird's eggs, designed to accompany egg-cups, that were a standard Macintyre range. Five of the eight pieces carry a Florian Ware mark. Jug height 11 ins

3

3 Group of wares decorated with sprays of roses, tulips and forget-me-nots, c1907. Vase height 9¼ ins
4 Group of wares decorated with poppies, tulips and contained panels of forget-me-nots, c1908–1909. For the brown version, see figure 3 on page 49. Largest vase height 9 ins

4

1 Group of wares decorated with the Eighteenth Century pattern, classical swags of roses and forget-me-nots, c1908. Trumpet vase height 10 ins

2 Group of wares decorated with a forget-me-not design contained within sharply incised panels, c1909. Largest vase height 8 ins

Macintyre Landscape Patterns, 1902-1913

The first Moorcroft landscape design, 397964, was registered in September 1902 and was included in the Florian Ware range. The characteristic design of trees in a rolling English landscape was first produced in shades of blue, with the tree heights varied to suit the shape of the vases. By the end of 1902 the green version was also in production and both were advertised in Liberty's *Yule-Tide Gifts* catalogue for that year, under the title Burslem Ware. The Liberty catalogue also mentioned the 'overglaze of yellow' that is a feature of many of the early landscape wares. Generally the Florian Ware mark is only found on the blue versions.

Liberty remained a major outlet for the landscape design, which was given the name Hazledene, and many pieces carry a Liberty mark However, the design was also sold through many other outlets. From about 1904 the colours gradually became richer and darker, culminating in the design of dark trees on an olive green ground that is typical of the period 1910-1913. This dark version of Hazledene was one of the patterns to be produced both at the Washington Works and at Cobridge, and so pieces carrying dates for 1913 and 1914 are quite common.

3 Two vases decorated with the landscape design, left a Florian Ware version in blue, right the green version with a Liberty mark, both c1903. Height 12 ins

4 Factory photograph of c1902, showing the landscape design on a Pompeian bowl.

1 Florian Ware vase decorated with the landscape design, c1902. Height 10 ins
2 Vase decorated with the landscape design, showing the blended blue, green and yellow colours, c1903. Height 12ins
3 Group of wares decorated with versions of the landscape design, showing varied tones of green and blue, c1903-1904. The ovoid vase on the left, the tall flared vase and the jug carry Florian Ware marks. Jug height 8ins

4

4 Group of wares decorated with the Hazledene landscape design in the colours associated with Liberty, including the typical 'overglaze of yellow', all c1903. Largest vase height 10ins

5 Group of wares decorated with the late, dark green version of the Hazledene landscape design, all carrying dates from 1912 to 1914. These show how the design was produced unchanged by Macintyre's and at Cobridge. Largest vase height 12¼ins

5

Liberty & Co and Lustre Wares

The close relationship between Liberty and Moorcroft had been established during the early days of Florian Ware and was based both on commerce and on the friendship between the Moorcroft and Liberty families. The Liberty backstamp had been in regular use on a number of designs since about 1901, and equally regular had been the appearance of many designs in the Liberty catalogues. Many lustres, including the ruby, feature in Liberty catalogues. Only one design, Bara Ware, was claimed to be exclusive, perhaps because of its links with Liberty fabrics, but many others have particular Liberty associations. Liberty never used Moorcroft's name during the Macintyre period as it was not their practise to reveal the names of designers or manufactures of wares made for them. Thus, although Florian Ware was sold under its own name, Liberty devised their own names for the later patterns, some of which later came into general use. These include the Hazledene landscape design, the Claremont toadstool design registered in October 1903, the Tudor Rose pattern registered in April 1904 and the pomegranate design introduced in 1910, and sold at first by Liberty under the trade name Murena. Liberty were also a major outlet for Moorcroft's first range to be decorated with monochrome and lustre glazes, the Flamminian Wares. These wares, with their bright red, green and blue streaked glazes and their Japanesque or Celtic foliate roundels, also featured lustre finishes for the first time. Registered in April 1905, Flamminian Wares were produced at least until 1915. By 1907 Moorcroft had developed other lustres, notably the ruby that was used over decoration outlined in slip, and he made extensive use of lustre glazes, both as monochromes and as a vibrant colour overlay for conventional patterns. Particularly notable are the wares with restrained floral decoration in a Japanese style and pale grounds washed with a luminous lustrous glaze, made from about 1907-1910.

1 Vase decorated with sprays of iris under a pale lustrous glaze, c1908. Height 9 ins
2 A part dinner service with a bluebell border, made for Liberty's and registered in 1904, design 431156
3 Public Record Office registration for the bluebell design, 431156 registered in 1904, inscribed: *The above drawing shews the design applied to a tea cup* (sic)

4 Group of vases decorated with roses, narcissi and prunus under pale lustrous glazes, c1908. Largest vase height 8 ins
5 Group of wares decorated with cornflowers, harebells, grapes and wisteria under pale lustrous glazes, c 1908. Largest vase height 8½ ins

1

2

3

1 Two vases with mottled lustre glazes over conventional designs, left a grape design with Liberty mark, right, roses made for Tiffany, New York, both c1909. Larger vase height 16 ins
2 Two vases, left decorated with a narcissi design under a pale lustrous glaze, right decorated overall with a scale pattern in Japanese style, made for Liberty, both c1907. Larger vase height 9½ ins
3 Vase decorated with a poppy design, the flowers, stems and handles picked out in red lustre, c1908. Height 6¾ ins
4 Group of wares decorated with the Bara design made from 1908–1913. Clock height 5½ ins
5 Group of wares decorated with the Bara Ware design, made from 1908–1913. Vase height 10 ins
6 Group of wares decorated with the Tudor Rose design, registered in April 1904. Plate diameter 7 ins

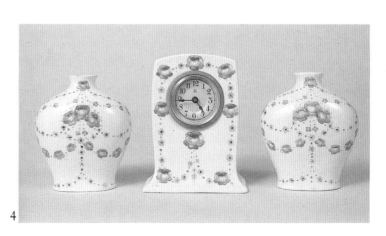

4

5

6

1 Group of Flamminian Ware showing the mottled glazes and the foliate roundels registered in April 1905. The green and red pieces carry Liberty marks and date from 1906-1913, while the blue vases were made at Cobridge in 1914. Coffee pot height 10 ins
2 Group of wares decorated with Hazledene, Claremont and prunus designs under a rich ruby lustre glaze. Ruby lustre was first produced in 1907. Largest vase height 10½ ins

3

3 Group of wares decorated with the Claremont toadstool design, registered in October 1903, showing the characteristic dark mottled grounds, and the stylistic similarities with the Hazledene landscape design. Most carry Liberty marks, and date from c1905. Largest vase height 13 ins
4 Group of wares decorated with the pomegranate design, introduced in 1910, showing the mottled yellow and green ground typical of early examples of this design. The vases are dated 1912 and carry Liberty marks. Vase height 9½ ins

4

Macintyre Tablewares, 1898-1913

Tablewares and domestic wares had always formed a significant part of Macintyre's output since the 1880s. Gesso Faience tableware, probably designed by Harry Barnard, was in production by 1896, and some were still being made in 1902. The tablewares designed and made under Moorcroft's direction fall into three categories. The first, the printed Aurelian wares, featured Moorcroft's designs from 1897, but were not made in his department. The second, the signed tableware, was made and decorated exactly as the art pottery, and featured many Moorcroft designs such as Florian, Hazledene, Claremont, blue poppy, Flamminian, Eighteenth century and pomegranate. The third category was the Dura Ware, made in Moorcroft's department, but with designs simplified to serve a wider market. A Macintyre tableware catalogue of 1902 illustrates five Dura Ware raised slip designs, credited to Moorcroft, three Aurelian Ware designs not credited to him, and a miscellaneous range of other domestic wares featuring conventional Macintyre styles and techniques of decoration. Three shapes, Guildhall, Edward and Kimberley, were also designed by Moorcroft and these are included alongside the earlier Persian, Lorne and Sicilian. The range of useful wares designed by Moorcroft was wide and included such things as teapot stands, moustache cups, covered muffins, marmalade jars, egg-cups, biscuit jars and salad bowls as well as many different sizes and styles of cups, plates and jugs. In 1902 a 29 piece breakfast set in Dura Ware, finished with best gold, cost £3.1s.0d. Some Dura Ware and Aurelian Ware remained in production until about 1914, and some of the designs were subsequently developed by Moorcroft for use on decorative wares. Moorcroft tableware was produced throughout the Macintyre period, and some of his shapes were registered as late as 1905.

Print from a glass negative of c1903 showing a Dura Ware daisy design on the Guildhall shape.

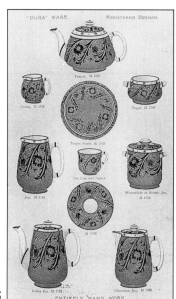

Pages from the Macintyre 1902 catalogue showing, 1, an Aurelian Ware printed design on the Lorne shape, 2, an Aurelian Ware printed design on the Persian shape, 3 Rococo style trays and dishes with Moorcroft decoration, 4, a Dura Ware raised slip design of poppies on the Edward shape, 5, a Dura Ware raised slip design on the Sicilian shape. Right, pages from the Macintyre 1902 catalogue showing, 6, an Aurelian Ware printed design on the Persian shape, 7, a selection of jug shapes decorated with conventional printed patterns, Aurelian Ware designs, standard Macintyre glazes, Gesso Faience and Dura Ware designs, 8, a Dura Ware raised slip seaweed design on the Guildhall shape, 9, a Dura Ware raised slip design on the Kimberley shape

6

7

8

9

1 Group of signed domestic wares decorated with Florian designs, including biscuit barrels, butter dishes, a scent bottle and a napkin ring, c1901. Larger biscuit barrel height 6 ins
2 Group of signed domestic wares decorated with Florian designs and featuring elaborate plated mounts, c1901. Salad server length 12ins
3 Group of signed domestic wares decorated with the Eighteenth Century design in different colour ways, all c1906. The tray, the ring stand and the pin box form part of a dressing table set. Tray width 13½ ins

3

4

5

4 Group of jugs and teapots decorated with simple floral designs and plain or coloured grounds, all c1903. The shapes of the yellow teapot and the white hot water jug were registered in January 1898. Tablewares of this type may be signed or unsigned. Coffee pot height 8 ins
5 Group of domestic wares showing versions of the printed Aurelian designs registered in February 1898, and a Dubarry dessert plate with a raised slip iris design, all c1902. These wares are generally unsigned, but signed examples of the Dubarry iris design have been noted. Larger jug height 8 ins

1 Group of Dura tableware with a poppy design registered in September 1902, on the Edward shape. Jug height 8½ ins

2 Group of domestic ware decorated with Florian designs, c1900–1902, all signed. Muffin dish diameter 7½ ins

3 Pieces from a teaset simply decorated with a border pattern from the 404017 design and a dark green ground, c1903, teapot signed. Teapot height 5½ ins

Two Macintyre catalogue pages of c1903 showing Dura Ware designs.

4

5

6

4 Selection of cups and saucers decorated with Florian, Dura, Eighteenth Century, pomegranate, Spanish and other designs, 1900-1914 (the yellow example is c1932).
5 Group of tobacco jars decorated with Florian and later designs, 1901-1906. All signed except the pink example.
6 Group of biscuit barrels decorated with Florian and later designs, showing different styles of plated mounts, 1900-1906. Mostly signed.

1 Teapot and bonbonnière decorated with the Claremont design, and additionally decorated with silver overlay and cut out silver leaves and flowers, c1905, made for Shreve & Co, San Francisco, Both signed. Teapot height 7 ins
2 Part of a tea service decorated with the Flamminian design, and additionally decorated with silver overlay and cut out silver leaves, c1905, all signed. Made for Shreve & Co, San Francisco. It is possible that the distinctive silver mounts shown on these wares were added in the United States. Teapot height 7 ins

3

4

3 Part of a tea service decorated with the Claremont design, c1905, all signed. Teapot height 6ins
4 Part of a tea service decorated with the cornflower design, c1911, all signed. Teapot height 6ins
5 Teapot decorated with the Claremont design, the shape registered in January 1905, made for Shreve & Co, San Francisco, signed. Height 5½ins
6 Unusual shape coffee pot with Claremont decoration and American silver mounts. Height 11ins

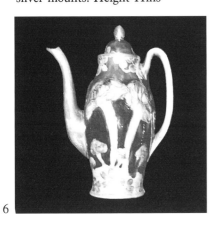

6

5

Chapter Three

The Move to Cobridge, 1913

Transitional Patterns, 1910-1918

In August 1913 Moorcroft moved to his newly built factory at Cobridge, on the outskirts of Burslem, accompanied by a small team of assistants, the craftsmen and women he had trained and who had worked with him at the Washington Works. The move was prompted by Macintyre's decision to concentrate on electrical porcelain. Within a few weeks, the production of Moorcroft pottery was once again under way. Moorcroft had announced his intention to form his own company and continue to make his pottery in his own workshops. While Liberty were particularly supportive, he was inundated with orders from other distributors, anxious to help his new venture during this critical period. It was essential to retain their confidence and meet the demand for the designs with which the buyers and the public were already familiar. He therefore continued at first to develop designs he had launched successfully between 1910 and 1912, the pomegranate, Spanish, brown Florian (chrysanthemum or revived cornflower) of 1910 and the pansy and wisteria of 1911. However, Liberty, among other distributors at home and overseas, still wanted the green Hazledene, the Claremont, the Flamminian ware, the Eighteenth Century and other designs characteristic of his work since 1908. As most of the pottery was made to order he was prepared to revive even earlier patterns when asked to do so. Yet despite the demand for his work, Moorcroft was shrewd enough to realise that his enterprise, run as a cottage industry in the Morris tradition, would be unable to survive on art pottery alone. He therefore began, immediately, to design a range of tableware that could be made in relatively large quantities and attract a wider market. The speckled blue table ware, that he called Blue Porcelain and which Liberty sold as Powder Blue, was first made in 1913, and became the vital backbone against which the art pottery would be developed.

During this transitional period, Moorcroft also continued his distinctive style of marking. For some years the Macintyre marks had been increasingly insignificant, and had vanished completely from many of the Liberty pieces. At the same time the Moorcroft signature had grown larger and more stylised. At Cobridge the signature became the main Moorcroft mark, supported by small impressed factory marks. Pieces made between 1912 and 1914 were often dated as well.

1 Group of pieces decorated with the revived cornflower or brown chrysanthemum design, showing the red flower on the mottled green ground. The narrow vase on the left and ashtray were made at Cobridge and are dated XI 1913, but all the others were made at Macintyre's. All c1912-1913. Tallest vase height 12¾ ins.

2

2 Group of pieces decorated with the revived cornflower design, showing yellow and purple flowers on pale green and cream grounds. Probably all made at Cobridge, c1913-1914. The trumpet vase in the centre and the bottle vase on the right are dated 1914. Tallest vase height 14½ ins

3 Two vases decorated with the revived cornflower design, showing the blue and the cream grounds. Both made at Macintyre's, c1912. Larger vase height 10 ins

4 Cornflower vase of unusual pink colouring. Made at Cobridge, c1914. Height 8 ins

5 Jardinière and stand decorated with the cornflower design. Made for the retailer George Anderson & Co. of Paisley c1912, a substantial firm of china and crystal merchants known to have existed at least until 1931. Both pieces carry Moorcroft's signature. Height 38 ins.

3

4

Pansy and Pomegranate Designs, 1910-c1938

Introduced in 1910 and 1911, the pomegranate and pansy designs marked a new stylistic departure for Moorcroft. Subtle and carefully balanced colours blending together over delicate slip trailing and pale or mottled grounds were the characteristic features of the new Moorcroft style. Decoration was limited to one area of the piece, usually an encircling band of pattern. The pomegranate design was drawn in an exotic and sensual style around the shoulder of the ware, while in the pansy and related wisteria designs of 1911/12 the flowers hung down from the rim. When first produced, these designs were sold extensively by Liberty, but their early success ensured the involvement of other retailers at home and abroad. In 1913 Moorcroft transferred the designs to his new factory and production continued almost without interruption. Pomegranate in particular became Moorcroft's most successful design, but both this and pansy remained in production until the late 1930s. During this period the designs were steadily changed. Early pomegranate, made between 1910 and the First World War, has a mottled yellow or green ground, but by 1916 these colours were already giving way to the deep purples and blues that dominated post war production. In the 1920s a simplified version was produced, with the fruit pattern contained between Art Deco bands. Pansy went through similar changes, the early white, ivory or celadon grounds giving way to dark blue from 1916. Because of their popularity, these designs were used extensively by Moorcroft and so can be found on all types of ware, including tablewares, with metal mounts and with flambé glazes.

1

2

1 Vase decorated with the pomegranate design, showing the mottled yellow ground. Made for Liberty at the Macintyre factory in c1912. Height 15 ins
2 Group of wares decorated with the pomegranate designs, showing the mottled green ground, all c1912-1913. Covered vase height 12¼ ins

1

1 Group of wares decorated with the pomegranate design, showing varied green and blue grounds, all 1913–c1925. The raised vase on the far right is dated X 1913. Plate diameter 10 ins.
2 Group of domestic wares decorated with the pomegranate design on mottled green grounds, 1912–1914. The clock and the candlestick were made at Macintyre's. The tall pot pourri is dated II 1914. Largest piece height 6½ ins

2

3 Group of vases decorated with various green flowers on green grounds, showing unusual transitional designs, 1912-1914. The trumpet vase was made at Cobridge, the others at Macintyre's. The smallest vase is dated 1912. Tallest vase height 14½ ins

4 Group of miscellaneous transitional wares decorated with the apple blossom design, showing different glaze finishes, 1912-1914. The red lustre basket and the trumpet vase were made at Macintyre's, the others at Cobridge. The Powder Blue handled vase is dated 1914. Basket height 5½ ins

5 Group of wares decorated with the wisteria design, showing the typical colours and style of drawing, 1912-1914. Tallest vase height 9½ ins

1 Group of wares decorated with the early version of the pansy design, showing the white and pale grounds. All made at Cobridge. The jug is dated 1916, the trumpet vase 1914. Jug height 14½ ins
2 Group of wares decorated with the early version of the pansy design, showing the white ground. All made at Macintyre's, 1911–1913. Tallest vase height 6¾ ins

3 Vase decorated with the pansy design, showing the mottled darker ground, c1918. Height 8¼ ins

4 Group of wares decorated with the early versions of the pansy design, showing white and pale green grounds. All made at Cobridge, 1913-1916. The footed bowl is dated 1914. Tallest vase height 8 ins

5 Group of wares decorated with the later versions of the pansy design, showing the dark grounds characteristic of the 1920s and the 1930s. The plate is dated 1923, the two narrow vases are 1920-1925, the two round vases c1935. Tallest vase 10¾ ins

Spanish and Claremont

Introduced in 1910, the Spanish design brought together two aspects of Moorcroft's work. The designs were drawn in the flowing, linear style typical of the Florian Wares, and still showed the influence of William Morris, but the colours had become much richer, featuring the dark reds, yellows, greens and blues associated with the pomegranate design. This lively and decorative pattern, drawn to cover the surface of the ware, incorporated a number of flower forms already used by Moorcroft, for example, iris, cornflower and tulip, but its colours make it quite distinctive. The design was made at both the Macintyre and Cobridge factories, and remained in production until the 1930s. Versions in other colours can occasionally be found, notably greens and blues.

The toadstool design, introduced in 1903 and named Claremont by Liberty, remained in use for nearly forty years. During the transitional period between 1913 and 1915, the design underwent comparatively little change, but by the 1920s the drawing had become bolder and the colours darker and stronger. The name Claremont was used loosely in Moorcroft's workrooms but was not applicable to the later toadstool and mushroom designs, when the motif was used under flambé or other decorative glazes in the 1920s and 1930s, or the simplified designs of the 1930s, painted in light colours on the pale matt grounds typical of the period.

2

3

4

5

1 Group of wares decorated with the Spanish design, showing the typical colours and the flowing patterns, all 1912–1916. The narrow vase bottom right is dated 1914. Tallest vase height 12½ ins
2 Covered jar decorated with a cornflower design in the Spanish colours, dated 1914. Height 14 ins
3 Vase decorated with a cornflower design in blue on a Powder Blue ground, similar in style to the covered jar, c1916. Height 13 ins
4 Goblet decorated with a version of the Spanish design showing a more open style of flower, c1912. Height 8¼ ins
5 Vase decorated with the Spanish design, c1916. Height 6¼ ins
6 Wares decorated with versions of the Spanish design. Left to right, a scent bottle in green, c1912, a vase with a simplified design on a mottled cream ground, c1930, and a vase with the conventional design, c1916. Cream vase height 5¼ ins

6

1

1 Group of wares decorated with the Claremont toadstool design, all 1913-1916. The tallest vase is dated 1914. Tallest vase height 12 ins

2 Group of wares decorated with the Claremont toadstool design, c1918. Candlesticks height 10 ins

2

3

3 Group of wares decorated with the Claremont toadstool design under flambé glazes, all c1930. Handled vase height 7¼ ins
4 Large vase decorated with the Claremont toadstool design in the typical colours of the transitional period, c1916. Height 13 ins
5 Group of wares decorated with late versions of the wisteria and toadstool designs, showing the simplified drawing, light colours and pale matt grounds of the mid 1930s. Both vases are dated 1935. Taller vase height 19½ ins

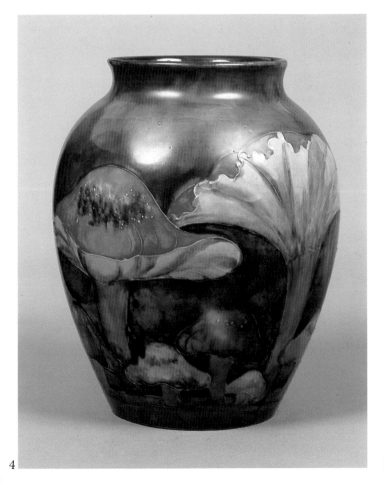

4   5

Chapter Four

Cobridge Productions, 1913-1945

Persian and Late Florian

While Moorcroft used some of his earlier designs at Cobridge, he embarked on fresh developments at the same time. The new designs reflected his desire both to move in new directions and to maintain the traditions he had established. Persian, introduced early in 1914, is an example of the former, while the Late Florian designs, developed during the First World War, are examples of the latter. Persian reflected the current enthusiasm for Middle Eastern styles of decoration and, although Moorcroft himself may not have been entirely satisfied with so untypical a design, it met a steady demand throughout the war and was not withdrawn until about 1920. The intertwined flowers that made up the pattern in strong colours on a pale ground were clearly inspired by Islamic tiles. Also partly Islamic in style were the range of wares featuring fruit and flower designs contained in panels on plain green, blue and grey grounds, produced between 1915-1916 and the early 1920s.

More characteristic was Moorcroft's continuing interest in Florian-style designs. Some of the early Florian designs had already been revived and redeveloped at the Macintyre factory between 1910 and 1912 and were to be revived again in a simpler and bolder form in the late 1920s and early 1930s. In between came the Late Florian designs, made during the early years at Cobridge and with a character of their own. The tightly drawn tulips, poppies, forget-me-nots and other flowers, the intricate surface patterns and the flowing forms of early Florian were still present, but the use of strong and rich colours created an entirely new effect. Similar colours were also used in a dramatic range of designs from about 1918 which featured narcissi, orchids, iris and other flowers drawn in a naturalistic style over the surface of the pots, often on dark grounds. Some of these designs may have been inspired by Thomas Moorcroft's botanical drawings. Lustre finishes were also used, another Macintyre tradition being maintained, while monochrome lustres were still an important part of Cobridge production.

1

2

3

4

1 Group of wares decorated with the Late Florian design, showing the characteristic blue, green and yellow colours and the decorative drawing style reminiscent of early Florian, all 1918-1923. The bowl is dated 1918. Larger vase height 14½ ins

2 Group of wares decorated with early and later versions of the Late Florian design, the vase on the left showing the simplification of the style that took place in the late 1920s and early 1930s. Left vase c1930, others c1920. Tallest vase height 11¾ ins

3 Large vase decorated with a rich version of the Late Florian design, dated 1919. Height 16 ins

4 Goblet and bowl decorated with the Persian design, 1914-1916. Bowl height 6¼ ins

5 Group of wares decorated with the Persian pattern, all 1914-1920. The tazza is mounted on a Liberty Tudric pewter base. Larger vase height 9½ ins

5

1

1 Vase decorated with an orchid design on a dark ground, perhaps inspired by Thomas Moorcroft's botanical drawings, dated 1919. Height 12¾ ins

2

2 Group of vases decorated with an orchid design on dark grounds, c1918. Largest vase height 13$\frac{1}{2}$ ins
3 Vases decorated with narcissus designs on mottled dark grounds, c1920. Larger vase height 11 ins
4 Vase decorated with a damson design on a mottled green ground, c1920. Height 11$\frac{1}{2}$ ins

3

4

1

1 Vase decorated with a cornflower design under a lustre glaze, dated 1918. Height 12½ ins
2 Group of wares decorated with plain lustre glazes, showing a range of colours, c1916. Green vase height 10½ ins

2

3

3 Group of wares with fruit and flower designs contained in panels on plain green and blue grounds, c1918. Trumpet vase height 9 ins
4 & 5 Covered jar and vase with forget-me-not and Persian designs contained in panels on powder blue grounds, c1918. Vase height 9½ ins

4

5

1

1 Group of wares decorated with the Moonlit Blue landscape design, c1925. Trumpet vase height 11 ins
2 Group of wares decorated with the Eventide landscape design, c1925. The trumpet vase and the inkwell have Tudric pewter mounts. Trumpet vase height 9 ins

2

Later Landscape Designs

One of Moorcroft's most characteristic developments during the early 1920s were the later landscape designs. After the move to the new factory the green landscape design, generally known by the Hazledene name given to it by Liberty, remained in production for a few years, probably until about 1916. In 1921 Moorcroft turned to landscape again as a source of inspiration and began to experiment with trees in blues and greens on a Powder Blue base. This culminated in the Moonlit Blue design, launched in 1922. A year later another landscape range was launched, Eventide with its rich oranges, reds and greens, and in about 1926 the third design appeared. This was Dawn, with its pale blue, white and yellow colours and a matt-finished surface. All three designs were similar in style to their predecessors, with rolling hills and tall, leafy trees but later other trees appeared, for example willows and others with more simplified forms. Landscape designs were continually popular and appeared on many shapes and in many forms throughout the 1920s and 1930s, including tablewares, large exhibition pieces, with silver, or silver on copper mounts and with flambé finishes.

4

3

5

3 Large vase decorated with the Moonlit Blue landscape design, with silver mounts by Francis Arthur Edwardes. Hallmark 1923. Height 17½ ins
4 Vase decorated with the landscape design in unusual colours and a light flambé glaze, c1928. Height 11½ ins
5 Group of vases decorated with toadstool and landscape designs in unusual colours. Left to right, mushrooms under a brown lustre glaze, c1910, signed but unmarked, a dark version of the Dawn design, c1928, and mushrooms in browns with a saltglaze finish, c1934. Largest vase height 11½ ins

1

1 Large vase and cover decorated with the Moonlit Blue landscape design, shown at the Wembley Exhibition in 1924, and a small Moonlit Blue vase to show the scale. Small vase height 3ins

2

3

2 Two vases decorated with a landscape design under flambé glazes, one with geometric borders, both c1928. Larger vase height 12 ins
3 Two vases decorated with versions of the landscape design in unusual colours, left a blend of Dawn and Moonlit Blue colours, c1932, right, a blend of Eventide and Moonlit Blue, dated 1929. Larger vase 18½ ins
4 Two vases decorated with landscape and grape designs in sombre saltglaze colours, c1928. Larger vase height 8½ ins
5 Vase decorated with the weeping willow landscape design, c1930. Height 14½ ins

4

5

1

2

3

1 Group of wares decorated with the Dawn landscape design, showing the variation of the colours under the matt glaze, c1928. Largest vase height 10½ ins

2. Two vases with a landscape pattern, chevron and scale borders, c1928. The blue example with a lustre glaze; the other has a red and purple colouring found at this period, distinct from Eventide. Taller vase height 9½ ins

3 Group of wares decorated with the weeping willow and weeping beech versions of the landscape design, c1930. Dish diameter 7 ins

Later Cornflower Designs

4 Group of Powder Blue wares decorated with a cornflower design, c1920. Largest vase height 12¼ ins
5 Group of wares decorated with cornflower designs in a wide range of colours, 1925-1935. Largest vase height 12½ ins

Domestic and Exotic Flower Designs

During the mid 1920s and early 1930s Moorcroft continued to use flowers as his main source of inspiration. At least ten new designs were produced during this period which featured a wide range of both domestic and exotic flora. This change of direction was marked by the appearance in about 1923 of the so-called big poppy design, which was derived directly from earlier Florian styles and, at the same time, a few earlier flowers, such as cornflower, orchid, poppy and wisteria, which Moorcroft particularly liked, had reappeared regularly in new forms or styles. However, in the late 1920s, a new series began to appear in which flowers were drawn in a direct style that was also botanically more accurate. English flowers were still the mainstay of Moorcroft's work, for example anemones, fresias, honeysuckle and other early summer plants, but there was an increasing interest in the exotic. The new orchid designs appeared, perhaps inspired by some of his father's botanical drawings, and then Moorcroft looked further afield for his ideas.

1 Group of wares decorated with the big poppy or anemone design, the two vases with flambé glazes c1929, the bowl and cover dated 1926. Larger vase height 10 ins
2 Group of wares decorated with the big poppy or anemone design on dark grounds, c1925. The trumpet vase has a Tudric pewter mount. Largest vase height 12¾ ins
2A Vase decorated with a poppy design on a powder blue ground, c1920. Height 12½ ins

1

2A

2

3

4

3 Vase decorated with the waratah design under a flambé glaze, c1932. Height 9½ ins
4 Plate decorated with the waratah design in natural colours, c1932. Diameter 8½ ins
5 Group of wares decorated with the waratah design, showing the version with a blue ground, c1932. Largest vase height 8¾ ins

5

1

2

5

1 Group of wares decorated with orchids and spring flowers, c1936.
Goblet height 10½ ins
2 Large vase decorated with the South African flower, *protea
cynaroides*, in natural colours, c1930. Height 11 ins
3 Group of vases decorated with late versions of the wisteria design,
two with dark blue grounds and the banded patterns of the late 1920s,
one in the typical pale matt colours of the mid 1930s, and one in a
revived Florian style, c1920. Largest vase height 13¼ ins
4 Group of warès decorated with a wisteria design on dark grounds,
1920-1925. Largest vase height 9¾ ins
5 Vase decorated with a version of the wisteria design, dated 1920.
Height 15 ins

3

4

1

1 Group of wares decorated with grape and leaf and blackberry and leaf designs, showing a range of colours, and including an unusual all-blue version, 1928-1935. Vase height 7½ ins

2 Group of wares decorated with an orchid design, showing a range of colours. Larger vase height 10¾ ins

2

3

4

3 Two vases decorated with the anemone design in different colours, c1938. Larger vase height 9½ ins
4 Lamp base decorated with a late version of the cornflower or chrysanthemum design, c1936, and a plate decorated with a honeysuckle design, c1936. Plate diameter 10ins
5 Group of wares decorated with a fresia design, in three colour versions, c1935. Larger vase height 12 ins

5

Later Fish Designs

During the Florian period, Moorcroft had used fish designs for some of his most splendid wares. Large jardinières and Hesperian vases were often decorated with carp drawn in a free and distinctly Japanese style. In the late 1920s fish reappeared, and continued to feature throughout the 1930s. However, these designs are very different. The Japanese element has disappeared, and the fish, now of less definable species, float freely over the surface of the ware, unencumbered by surrounding weeds and swirls. Many of the fish even have a cartoon quality, and on some pots this because quite surreal, with garden plants growing quite happily underwater beneath the fish. The occasional jellyfish or octopus adds excitement. Mostly drawn in greens and blues, the fish designs were often given a flambé glaze. Others occur in paler colours under matt magnolia glazes on the distinctive shapes of the late 1930s.

1A

1

1A Vase decorated with a fish and seaweed design, c1913, mentioned in a letter to Alwyn Lasenby in January 1913. Height 10½ ins

1 Group of wares decorated with fish designs in typical colours, c1930–1936. Largest vase height 19¾ ins

2 Group of wares decorated with a fish design under matt glazes, c1930. Largest vase height 16 ins

2

3

4

3 Dish decorated with a fish design under a flambé glaze, c1930. Diameter 11 ins
4 Large vase decorated with a fish design, dated 1931. Height 18¾ ins
5 Group of wares decorated with fish designs in typical colours, some with flambé glazes, all c1930 except the vase on the far right which is dated 1933. Largest vase height 14½ ins

5

Flambé Wares, 1919-1945

In common with many of his contemporaries, for example, Bernard Moore, Charles Noke and Howson Taylor, Moorcroft developed an interest in transmutation and other orientally-inspired high temperature glazes in the early 1900s. He lacked the facilities to develop his own flambé glazes at the Macintyre factory and, during the First World War, at Cobridge, but in 1919 he decided to build a special kiln for the purpose. It was not completed until 1921 but by 1922 Moorcroft was already producing his first rouge flambé glazes, and using them either without additional ornament for a plain flambé ware, or as an overlay on ware that had been decorated in his usual style. During the next two decades Moorcroft became a master of the flambé process, and some of his most spectacular pieces were decorated by means of this complex and demanding technique. He never attempted to standardise his effects. He enjoyed the extraordinary blend of skill and chance that made every example of this flambé ware unique, exploiting to the full the range of rich reds, yellows and browns, shot with other colours, that could be obtained when the process was used successfully. He controlled the glazing and the firing of the ware himself, firing his kiln alone, and carefully nursing it through the vital transmutation process unaided. By this personal control, he was able to develop the wide range of flambé colours and finishes that were compared by experts with the sang de boeuf and other monochrome glazes of the early Chinese potters. Although many of his finest pieces were devoid of ornament other than the glaze itself, he achieved equally dramatic results by using the flambé as an overglaze when flowers, fruit, foliage, toadstools and landscapes loomed through an overlay of rich red, chartreuse and other colours. Moorcroft received many accolades for his flambé glazes and continued to experiment with this exacting process until his death in 1945. He guarded his secrets jealously, revealing them only to his son, Walter Moorcroft, who developed his own flambé ware after his father died.

1A

1A Vase decorated with a poppy design under a flambé glaze, with decorative metal mounts by Francis Arthur Edwardes, c1925

1

1 Group of wares decorated with flambé glazes over a range of designs, including blackberry and leaf, waratah, big poppy, pomegranate, peacock feather and wheat, 1925-1935. Bowl diameter 9¼ ins
2 Vase decorated with an even rouge flambé glaze in Chinese style, with silver cover and foot by Francis Arthur Edwardes, c1926. Height 10¼ ins

2

3

3 Owl standing on a rock, cast from a model by the artist and silversmith, Francis Arthur Edwardes, decorated by Moorcroft, in rouge flambé glaze. Edwardes modelled a very limited number of pieces, including animals, birds and grotesque masks that were treated in this way. Very few of them were made, and were seldom repeated. They were sold as individual pieces, or even unique examples of the pottery, but were not reproduced for general sale, about 1925. Height 8½ ins
4 Vase decorated with the Eventide design between bands of chevrons, with a light flambé glaze, c1925. Height 9½ ins
5 Lamp decorated with the wisteria design under a rich flambé glaze, c1925

4

5

1 Group of vases decorated with the wisteria design under flambé glazes, c1928. Largest vase height 9½ ins

2 Group of wares decorated with a fresia design under flambé glazes, showing different intensities of red, c1934. Bowl diameter 12 ins

3

3 Group of wares decorated with leaves and fruit designs under flambé glazes, 1928-1934. Dish diameter 10 ins

4 Group of wares decorated with fish designs under flambé glazes, 1930-1938. Bowl diameter 7½ ins

4

2

3

1 Vase decorated with the toadstool design under a flambé glaze, c1932. Height 13 ins
2 Tall vase decorated with the waratah design under a rich flambé glaze. Dated 1933. Height 18½ ins
3 Vase decorated with a fish design under a flambé glaze, c1938. height 14½ ins
4 Charger decorated with the pomegranate design, under a rich ruby flambé glaze, c1925. Diameter 15½ ins

4

Miscellaneous Wares

Moorcroft always considered that the design and production of useful ware was as important as ornamental pieces. The backbone of this production throughout the 1920s and 1930s, and indeed until the early 1960s was the Moorcroft Blue tableware. During this period, other plain tablewares were produced, notably the yellow Sunray version, introduced in 1933 and made until 1939, and advertised in Liberty catalogues during the late 1930s. Decorative tableware, featuring most of the ornamental designs and fully signed, was also produced. While some plates and plaques were clearly ornamental, decorative tablewares were designed for the Moorcroft Blue shapes, but some interesting forms, inspired by Middle Eastern and oriental pottery and designed at Macintyre's, were used until about 1916. The useful wares were expanded to include dressing table sets, trays, mugs, candlesticks, beads, buttons and the characteristic square biscuit boxes. Ware designed to be mounted in silver, silver plate, pewter and other metals was also produced until the

1930s, maintaining the tradition established at Macintyre's since 1898. These included teasets, ashtrays and smoker's sets, inkwells and many other articles, including little plaques to be mounted as brooches. Moorcroft began to make miniature pieces at Macintyre's, at a time when miniature vases, jugs and beakers were popular, and production continued at Cobridge, along with small scent bottles and trinket boxes. These little pieces called for a delicacy of touch, taxing the skills of the designer, the potter and the decorator, and were therefore quite expensive to make.

1

2

1 Group of domestic and tablewares decorated with a wisteria design, some with metal mounts, c1925. Teapot height 6 ins
2 Part of a teaset decorated with the green Hazledene landscape design, showing Middle Eastern forms designed at Macintyre's, made at Cobridge, c1916. Teapot height 10 ins
3 Group of useful wares decorated with the Moonlit Blue landscape design, and showing various metal mounts, c1924. Teapot height 5½ ins
4 Group of tablewares decorated with the pomegranate design, 1915–1930. Tray width 10½ ins
5 Group of tablewares decorated with the pansy design, some with metal covers, c1914. Larger jug height 5 ins

3

4

5

1

2

3

4

5

1 Group of cups and saucers decorated with various designs, including pomegranate, toadstool and leaf and fruit. The example on the far left has a flambé glaze, 1915-1930. Cup height 3 ins
2 Group of mugs, showing a range of shapes and decorative styles, including conventional patterns, saltglaze and slipwares, 1914-1935. Tallest height 4$^{1}/_{2}$ ins
3 Group of biscuit boxes decorated with pomegranate, Hazledene, poppy, pansy and Claremont designs, three dated 1914. Height 6 ins
4 Monochrome tableware showing early pink, pale blue celadon, c1914, also sunburst yellow, purple, pale lustre on powder blue, from 1920. Coffee pot height 6 ins
5 Group of plates decorated with a range of designs and glazes, 1914-1930. Largest diameter 7 ins

1

1 A selection of powder blue tableware showing some rare items including a moustache cup and a ring tree. The variations in the tone and speckling of the blue can be seen. Height of candlestick (right hand) 8 ins

2 Selection of miniature vases, bowls, jugs and loving cups, and a scent bottle, decorated with a wide range of Moorcroft designs, including Aurelian, Florian, Flamminian, landscape, toadstool, Spanish, Persian, pomegranate, various floral patterns and flambé glazes. 1898-1935. Average height 2¼-4 ins

3 Traveller's fitted case containing examples of the Moorcroft Blue and Sunray tablewares, c1935

4 Plate decorated with chevrons and carrying the words MOORCROFT POTTERY, one of a small number of designs made for exhibition and display purposes between 1913 and the mid 1920s and not offered for general sale. Diameter 10½ ins

5 Selections of buttons, knobs, beads and metal mounted brooches, decorated with various Moorcroft designs and lustre glazes, 1914-1925

2

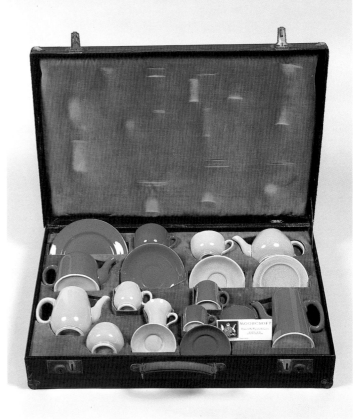

3

4

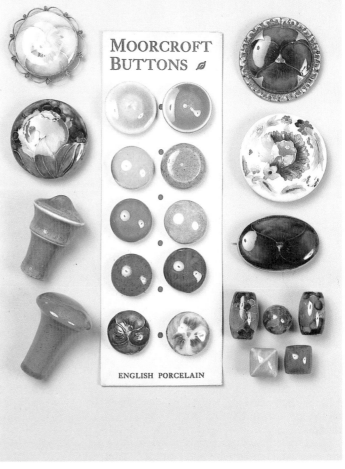

5

1930s Designs

The 1930s were a difficult time for Moorcroft, partly because of the international financial situation, and partly because of changing attitudes towards decorative pottery. The bright colours of the 1920s had been replaced by pale and sombre tones, and decorative patterns had given way to the plain, handcrafted styles of the studio potter. Moorcroft, always alert to changes in contemporary taste, responded in a number of ways. First, his export market was still strong and so he continued to develop his floral designs and flambé glazes. Second, he expanded tableware production, introducing the yellow Sunray and a plain green range. Third, he introduced new designs that reflected the taste for lighter and more subdued colour, matt glazes and abstract or geometric ornament. Some incorporated highly simplified versions of earlier motifs, such as peacock feather or honesty, while others were entirely new, for example yacht, orange and blossom or waving corn. It was a period of experiment and many other designs appeared on individual pieces but were not developed further.

By late 1930s Moorcroft was incresingly in competition with the studio potters and it must have been ironical for him, whose pottery had always been thrown, turned and decorated by hand, to have to produce wares whose finish emphasised the handcraft look. He developed what he called 'natural pottery' whose new and unsophisticated style was in stark contrast to the Moorcroft tradition for excellence in finish. The lathe was dispensed with, and the ware was finished on the wheel with ribbing and primitive banding. None of the shapes were standardised, some remaining as they left the wheel, while others were formed into eccentric shapes by squeezing or manipulation. Pale colours or the semi-matt magnolia glazes were used to finish the ware, sometimes over the simple slip designs. 'Natural pottery' was sold at home and abroad but it was not particularly successful. Pieces were generally regarded as 'not typically Moorcroft', but some were commended, in Canada and elsewhere, for their oriental simplicity and spontaneity.

1

2

1 Three vases decorated with a leaves and fruit design, showing the simplification of the decoration during the 1930s. Left, a flambé glazed version, centre, a full coloured version under light flambé glaze, right, a plain version with the design drawn in outline, 1930-1938.
Height 12½ ins
2 Three vases showing the development of the peacock feathers design, left, a Florian vase with the original design registered in 1899, centre, a revived Florian design of c1910, right, the simplified style of the late 1920s. Largest vase height 11¼ ins

3

3 Group of wares decorated with the peacock feather design, showing the simplified drawing and dark blue grounds developed at Cobridge, c1918. Bowl diameter 12½ ins
4 Group of wares decorated with a late version of the peacock feathers, showing the stylised drawing and banding characteristic of the 1930s, c1934. Largest vase height 12½ ins

4

1 Group of wares decorated with the simplified design and matt glazes of the 1930s, showing tulip and honesty patterns, c1935. The two vases with monochrome designs in panels also show the continuity of styles during this period, for the smaller dates from c1916, and the larger is dated 1941. Largest vase height 10½ ins

2 Vase decorated with the late version of the honesty design, c1932. Height 13 ins

3 Vase decorated with the waving corn design, showing clearly its development from the landscape patterns, c1934. Height 13 ins

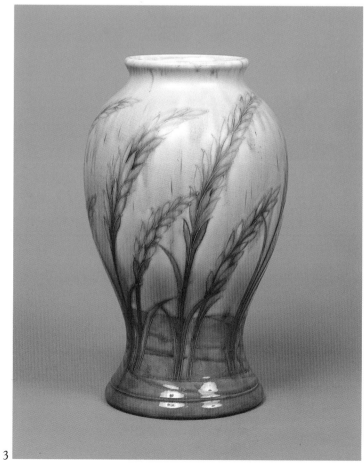

4

4 Group of wares decorated with the waving corn design, showing pale and mottled green grounds, ovoid vase dated 1937. Tallest vase height 14 ins
5 Group of wares decorated with simplified 1930s designs, the dish and jug with the orange and blossom pattern, the vase with flowers and fruit, all c1935. Jug height 8½ ins

5

1

2

3

1 Yacht pattern dinner and tea ware. A variety of different treatments. Diameter of plate 10 ins
2 A selection of matt and gloss colourways associated with the yacht pattern. Diameter of green matt plate, 8¼ ins
3 Group of 1930s tableware, the vase and jug with slip-coloured outlines for the patterns. Cup with peacock eye. Height of two handled vase 6½ ins
4 Group of wares decorated with the yacht design in various colourways, and a plate with a duck design, 1934-1938. Larger vase height 10 ins
5 Group of wares decorated with the simplified Art Deco version of the peacock feathers design, with typical ribbing and matt finish, c1938. Jug height 10 ins

4

5

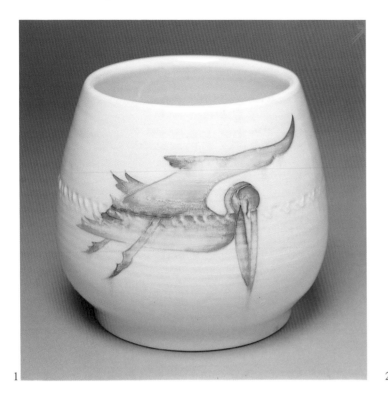

1 'Natural pottery' vase decorated with a pelican design in pale colours on a matt magnolia glaze, c1938. Height 4$^{1/2}$ ins
2 Vase with abstract, slip-trailed design, signed W. Moorcroft. Several of these vases were made and presumably marketed. Height 6 ins
3 Monochrome and mottled pieces, yoyo natural ware, black bowl and vase with legs on powder blue base, c1930. Tallest 8 ins
4 Group of 'natural pottery' decorated with monochrome glazes, showing the characteristic handcrafted forms and simple ribbed surface patterns, c1935-1939. Height of blue lustre vase 9$^{1/4}$ ins

Design Supplement

Illustrated below is a selection of wares decorated with designs by William and Walter Moorcroft that have come to light since the publication of the first edition of this book in 1987.

1 Recently discovered rare Florian Ware vase with the yacht design and butterfly border, c1900. Height 10ins (see page 10)
2 Florian Ware lamp base decorated with a tulip design, c1902. Height 13ins
3 Pompeian shape vase in Florian Ware, decorated with chrysanthemums and tulips, c1903. Height 10ins
4 Two Florian Ware vases decorated with an honesty design, with the typical roughened surface, c1903. Larger vase 9ins

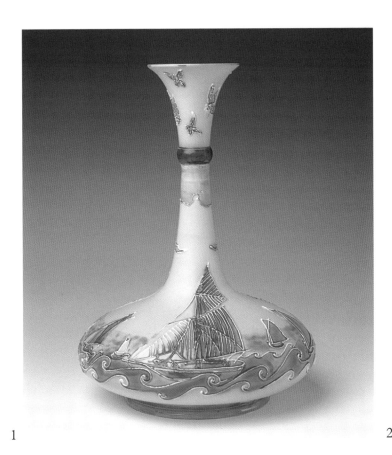

1

2

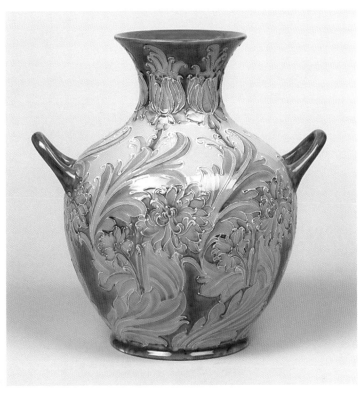

3

4

1

2

1 Bowl decorated with Florian style designs in blue and green, c1902. Diameter 12½ ins

2 Two Florian Ware vases, left with the lilac design in unusual colours and right a tulip design made for Liberty's, c1904. Larger vase height 12½ ins

3 Vases decorated with Florian designs in blue, green and yellow, both made for Liberty's, c1903. Larger vase height 5 ins

4 Group of Florian Wares decorated with blue, green and yellow designs, c1903. The two taller vases made for Liberty's. Height 7½ ins

3

4

5 Vase and covered jar decorated with the Persian pattern, showing two ground colours, c1916. Vase height 7½ ins
6 Pair of dishes with the wisteria and pomegranate patterns and silver plated mounts. Diameter 5 ins
7 Dish with wisteria pattern and Tudric Art Nouveau pewter mount. Diameter 11 ins
8 Vase decorated with an unusual version of the landscape design, the trees against a dramatic black sky c1926. Height 10½ ins
9 Vase decorated with an unusual version of an orchid design with a matt salt glazed finish c1928. Height 12½ ins
10 Vase decorated with an Art Deco peacock design, c1935. Height 9½ ins

1

2

3

1 Covered jar decorated with a Dura Ware design on the Kimberley shape, c1902. Height 7 ins
2 Cup and saucer unusually decorated with a classical design of Flamminian-style roundels linked by daisy chains, richly gilded, c1908. Height 2¹/₂ ins
3 Cup and saucer decorated with the Tudor Rose design, made for Liberty, c1905. Height 2¹/₂ ins
4 Walter Moorcroft vase decorated with a tiger lily design on a yellow ground, showing both sides of the flower. Dated 2.12.64. Height 13¹/₄ ins
5 Walter Moorcroft hedgevine vase, inspired by bryony found growing in the hedgerows of Worcestershire. Introduced in 1960 and only made for a short time on this shape.

4

5

Walter Moorcroft at Cobridge, 1935-1987

Walter Moorcroft was born on 12 February 1917. After attending a preparatory school in Buxton, he went to Rugby, leaving at the age of 18. At that point his father gave him a choice; he could either continue his education at university, or he could come into the works. Walter did not hesitate in making his decision and started at Cobridge directly from school in 1935. The next four years were a vital period of development for him, giving him an insight into every aspect of pottery design, manufacture and selling. He became familiar with his father's working methods and the characteristic features of every design and so, although he received no formal design or art education, he was able to produce his own experimental designs during the late 1930s.

When the Second World War broke out Walter continued to work with his father at Cobridge until he was called up for military service, when he was recommended to serve with the Intelligence Corps. When his father collapsed with a stroke at the end of September 1945 Walter was released from service in Germany on compassionate leave and was subsequently demobilised. His experiences from 1935 to his joining the army enabled him to take immediate responsibility for the running of the factory.

In his first year back at Cobridge Walter appointed company accountants, cleared all outstanding losses and showed a satisfactory profit. He re-joined the British Pottery Manufacturers Federation, from which his father had resigned in the 1930s following a disagreement, and was cordially welcomed by its directors. This was an important move as the pottery industry was at this time subject to numerous controls and the Federation not only represented the interests of manufacturers but was also in many cases responsible for the implementation of the government controls, notably the issuing of licences for the sale of decorated 'export rejects' in the home market. The sale of best quality decorated pottery and porcelain in the home market was prohibited until 1952 but the demand from overseas was almost unlimited. Apart from the traditional markets, Moorcroft

1

2

1 Large vase decorated with a fighting cock under a rich flambé glaze, designed by Walter Moorcroft in 1938. Based on a Chinese illustration, this was one of Walter's earliest identifiable designs and about 6 were made in different finishes. The vase carried William's signature. Height 12 ins

2 Charger decorated with a poppy design by Walter Moorcroft under a rich flambé glaze, c1939, and signed by William. Diameter 16¾ ins. Both these pieces date from the end of Walter Moorcroft's period of training at Cobridge and show him starting to develop a distinctive personal style. Further progress in this direction was cut short by the outbreak of war in 1939

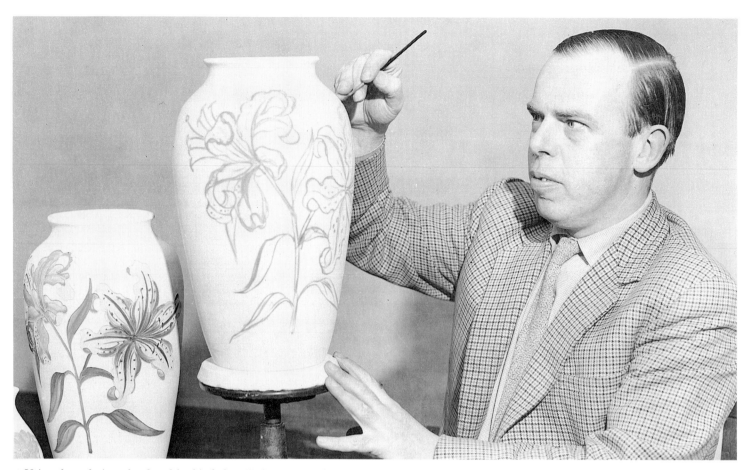

1 Using the technique developed by his father, Walter Moorcroft sketches a lily design directly onto the pot. For the completed design on a vase, see page 138

received orders during this period from many unexpected places such as Bogota, Columbia, Guatemala and Papua and New Guinea. Walter's association with the Federation was limited only by his commitments at the factory, and he served for a number of years on the Advisory Committee of Art, the function of which was the liason between manufacturers and the local Schools of Art.

While his father's designs had been vital during the difficult period of transition from 1945 to 1950, Walter soon began to develop his own style. His early patterns such as columbine and clematis tended to follow in his father's footsteps, but more distinctive and personal styles began to emerge during the 1950s. From the start, the exotic appealed more to Walter than to his father, reflected both in the more dramatic use of colour and the choice of subjects such as hibiscus and arum lily, and much later Bermuda lily, Caribbean and marine designs.

Walter's greatest inheritance from his father was his under-standing of the transmutation process. Walter continued the experiments in flambé firing that he had started before the war. William had always kept the secrets of his flambé process to himself, preparing his own glazes and firing the kiln but, during the vital four year period before the war, he had transmitted these to Walter. During the late 1940s and early 1950s Walter was able to complete his mastery of this complex and dramatic technique, and he showed himself to be as dedicated to its harsh disciplines as his father had been before him. By expanding the use of silver in the firing alongside the more usual copper, he was able to increase the range of flambé colours, adding bright yellow to the reds, greens and browns, and control the application of the flambé colours to the details of the designs. Walter pushed the flambé process to its limits, making the most of its potential for unexpected accidental effects. It was a demanding and time consuming process. To achieve the rich colours sometimes required two glaze firings followed by up to three flambé firings, at intervals of three weeks. Firing too often could destroy the colours. The results were always unpredictable, and rarely

repeatable. Even the weather was important: 'I always licked my finger to see which way the wind was blowing before firing', says Walter. Flambé firing continued at Cobridge until 1970, when the arrival of natural gas made it no longer practical and the oven was finally pulled down in 1973. At its peak flambé represented 10% of the output.

At the Festival of Britain in 1951, Blue Porcelain tableware was selected for exhibition, along with two small ox blood flambé bowls shown in the special pavilion. In 1957 and 1958 Blue Porcelain was also selected for display at the Design Centre. In 1956 the first bottle oven was demolished following the installation of the first electric tunnel kiln for glaze firing, and the change over to electric firing was completed in 1960. The second bottle oven was then demolished but the third was retained to become an historic feature of the factory. This expensive modernisation programme caused the company to make losses for a short time.

Throughout this period Liberty's retained their financial interest in the company, but a restructuring of the Board and the shareholding in 1947 had given the Moorcroft family joint control and equal voting rights. Walter, as Chairman, had the casting vote, and so the Liberty influence was restricted. The relation-ship, if rather negative by this time, remained cordial, but was limited to the Annual General Meeting, held each December with courteous ceremony in Liberty's London boardroom, preceded by an invitation to Walter to join the Liberty directors for lunch in their private dining room.

By 1960 Liberty's felt that the continuation of their connection with Moorcroft served little purpose and so they offered their shares to the Moorcroft family on favourable terms. The transfer took place early in 1961, achieved by the capitalisation of the reserve fund to increase the company's capital value by £5000. All the A and B shares were then withdrawn, to be replaced by ordinary £1 shares with Walter holding 6250 and Beatrice and Hazel, William's widow, 1250 each. Beatrice and Hazel Moorcroft also became directors at this point.

3 Queen Mary, a keen buyer of Moorcroft for over thirty years, continued her habit of visiting the Moorcroft stand at the British Industries Fair after William's death. Here, she examines a pot with Walter Moorcroft in 1947

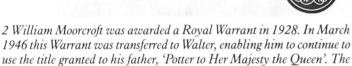

2 William Moorcroft was awarded a Royal Warrant in 1928. In March 1946 this Warrant was transferred to Walter, enabling him to continue to use the title granted to his father, 'Potter to Her Majesty the Queen'. The Warrant expired in 1978, 25 years after the death of Queen Mary

4 Placer W. Bowler loads a sagger into the oven in 1952 while Walter Moorcroft and Geoffrey Lloyd, Minister of Fuel and Power, look on

5 The decorating room in 1954

In 1962 John Moorcroft, Walter's half-brother, joined the company. Educated at Rugby School, he had graduated from Oxford University in 1959, and then spent three years on data processing at ICT, a period that put him in touch with a number of large companies and gave him valuable experience in business management. Apart from assisting with a number of developments within the factory, John took over primary responsibility for sales and marketing. His entry into the company came as a great help to Walter who had run the business single-handed for seventeen years. In 1977 John was given a small block of previously unissued shares and became a director.

Walter Moorcroft was in charge at Cobridge for over forty years and throughout much of this time he was entirely responsible for every aspect of the factory's production from design to distribution. Under his control the factory has maintained its reputation as a small industrial studio pottery, relying largely on traditional skills and crafts. Certain technical changes have occurred, for example casting has replaced throwing, but essentially the factory is still one where William would feel at home. As a designer Walter has made his mark but, once again, the styles and methods developed by his father have been maintained. Slip-trailing and hand decoration have continued, ensuring that Moorcroft pottery has a distinctive quality that can be recognised anywhere in the world. While relying largely on natural inspiration for his designs, Walter has been wide-ranging in his use of sources. Some patterns were based on flowers he found in his garden, or leaves picked up on the golf course, while others have been inspired by plants he found during visits to the Caribbean and other exotic or distant countries. Perhaps the most adventurous period was the 1960s and early 1970s, a time when Walter's initial dependence upon his father's later designs came to end, and when his own skill as a designer reached maturity. This period also coincided with a great change in his personal life for in 1959 he married again, his first wife having died in tragic circumstances several years before. His new enthusiasm for life was reflected by the bright colours and dynamic styles that marked the 1960s. In the mid 1970s Walter brought about another change when he designed the magnolia range, a complete break with traditional Moorcroft colouring that established a pattern for the future.

For over seventy years the Moorcroft pottery remained a family business, controlled first by William from 1913 to 1945 and then by Walter from 1945 to 1984. In 1984, John became Managing Director and at the same time the Moorcroft family sold a controlling interest in the shares of W. Moorcroft Limited to three brothers, Michael, Stephen and Andrew Roper, whose extensive interests in ceramics included the Churchill Group. Under the shrewd eye of Roper management, production techniques were streamlined. A range of wares with moulded decoration was introduced to increase production, featuring geranium and campanula designs by Walter.

The elimination of many shapes and decorations in the interests of standardisation and volume growth was logical in business terms, even if it seemed a radical departure from the Moorcroft tradition. Moorcroft became a very small cog in a much larger corporate machine, but the Ropers tried to give it a flagship status within the Churchill Group, a decision influenced both by their enthusiasm for the wares and by a family friendship with John Moorcroft that had started on the hockey field. However, enthusiasm and friendship were not enough and the hoped-for volume market did not appear. As a result the Roper Brothers' involvement proved to be short-lived and in September 1986, following John Moorcroft's wishes in the matter, they sold their shareholding in W Moorcroft Limited to the Dennis and Edwards families.

6 *Adrienne Moss painting a lily design in 1954*

7 *Thrower Ted Burden at work, 1954*

8 *Turner Fred Pickstock at work, 1954*

Reflections on Half a Century
of Moorcroft

In June 1989 Walter Moorcroft talked to the members of the Moorcroft Collectors' Club and reminisced about his experiences working with his father in the 1930s and about his life with Moorcroft until his retirement in 1987. Containing as it does so much information, this is now reproduced, with Walter Moorcroft's permission to mark the transition between his father's work, and his own.

Almost as soon as I could walk, my mother used to bring me up the works, as it was always known. The word factory was too commercial.

I have scant memories of these visits except for my extreme dislike of being kissed by the ladies in the decorating room.

I entered the business in 1935 after leaving school rather than go to university as business was far from good and my father's health had suffered in consequence.

After the enormous success of the 1920s Moorcroft fell out of favour in the 1930s owing to the general antipathy to traditional styles of decoration.

Modern was the key to acceptance and favourite colours were oatmeal and white. It gave me great satisfaction in the later 1930s to read a comment in a New York journal that the White Walls of Modernism were Collapsing like the Walls of Jericho.

Fortunately, we continued to have loyal support from our customers overseas specially in Canada, Africa and Australia and our Blue Porcelain was universally accepted.

For the first three years I worked without pay from the company. This was hardly slavery as my father provided me with a first class season ticket on the railway, lunch daily at the Grand Hotel, Hanley, not to mention membership of Trentham Golf Club with financial support to enter all the competitions, and I won my fair share.

We travelled to work from Trentham railway station and then by the loop line which ran from Stoke – Etruria – Hanley – Waterloo Road – Cobridge – Burslem and all stations to Macclesfield where it re-joined the main line.

At lunch time we took the train from Cobridge to Hanley where the Grand Hotel was alongside the station and it took ten minutes to get there. Having had a good half hour for lunch, I would return to Cobridge on the 1.25 train and my father would follow on the 1.40, proud of the the fact that he could have a quick sleep between Hanley and Cobridge without ever being carried past the station.

My father's working methods were a law unto themselves and he insisted that I learned my potting the Moorcroft way rather than risk contamination from the commercial methods taught at the local technical college. There was probably more wisdom in this than meets the eye as his way of working was often quite contrary to the procedure regarded as standard in industrial potting.

I soon concluded that the secret of Moorcroft processes often lay in their unorthodox simplicity.

Secrecy was an operative word and my father would invariably have bags of material stacked on the office floor for safe keeping. He bought his ingredients from different suppliers, so that no one supplier could find out what he was using by referring to his invoices.

My father's unorthodox methods were typified by an incident I shall always remember. There was no electricity on the factory and oil lamps were used when cleaning out the flues of the bottle ovens. My father was experimenting with plain glazes and emptied the oil from the nearest lamp into a vat of coloured glaze, to obtain a variegated effect. It worked remarkably well.

Initially my main function on the works was one of observation. The week started with watching the drawing or emptying of the bottle oven on Monday morning. The saggars full of ware were passed down by a team of men inside the oven and they were emptied by a team of women on the ground. I checked the results of the firing in relation to the part of the oven in which the ware had been placed. Different colours had to be placed in different parts of the oven according to the temperature required. When the oven was emptied I would go inside to make sure that any damaged pieces had not been conveniently lost in the ashes.

The firing varied every week. Sometimes there was a "bad oven" which meant a bad day with a full pitched row between my father, the fireman and the placer, often resulting in the placer receiving seven days notice, which was invariably rescinded before the end of the week.

As my experience increased observation gradually changed to management. I soon discovered that the surest way of implementing an idea of mine was to present it to my father as impossible, which would bring immediate contradiction and instruction to carry on as planned. With the help of such ploys I was able to relieve my father of a lot of the petty details of management and daily routine, with the result that between 1937 and 1939 he found time and inspiration for fresh creative work.

When I arrived at the factory the backbone of our production was still pansy, pomegranate and wisteria with autumn leaves as a vehicle for the flambé firing. The pansy, pomegranate and wisteria were all on a dark blue background, whereas the autumn leaves, prior to the reduction firing were on a green background. This appealed to a number of people as a change from the blue and quite a lot was sold in this way. So you had autumn leaves flambé, and autumn leaves to which was added at a later date blue leaf at the special request of a Canadian customer.

In 1937 the orchid and anemone provided a much needed change from the decorating which went back to the 20s. The orchid was the result of my father going to the Paris Exhibition in 1937, backed up with a very fine early colour photograph sent to him from Australia by the head of the Aspro Company, showing a wide variety of orchids grown in his greenhouses. These were followed by spring flowers and African lily both of which were inspired by beautifully illustrated menu cards of the Union Castle Mail Steamship Company, brought over by a South African customer.

Clematis was done about 1939 from flowers growing in our garden at Trentham. This was only done on a few pieces and it was not until after World War Two that I developed it into a complete range.

With the outbreak of War in September 1939 survival became the order of the day. I was above the age for immediate call-up and was able to help my father for a while. It was however a great relief to me when I was called-up for military service. As I had a working knowledge of three languages, I was drafted into Intelligence, which proved invaluable when my father collapsed in September 1945, as I was close to Army Headquarters and receiving the news on a Saturday morning, I was put on a freight aircraft on Sunday and took-over the business on Monday morning. My father lived for two weeks but was unable to speak.

In closing this chapter, I would like to pay tribute to the enormous tenacity which my father displayed in keeping the factory going single-handed through those war years. At least he knew that I was back and all set to carry on.

In my father's lifetime art work was his sole prerogative and although I was allowed to produce one or two pieces these were not recognised as part of the Moorcroft production. My first contribution to Moorcroft I designed while still at school in the form of a vase to commemorate the Silver Jubilee of King George V in 1935.

Other pieces that I did before the War were a round covered bowl with a single tiger lily - one of which was bought by the Duchess of Gloucester - one or two roughly drawn birds on roughly made vases and the most impressive item a bantam fighting cock on a large spherical vase, one of which was completed in flambé colours and is illustrated in the Moorcroft Book.

I received no art training as my father had contempt for the styles currently in vogue for Art School teaching.

I was fortunate in having had very good art masters at Rugby, where I was also a member of the sketching club. It was in fact in my study at school that I made the working drawings for the tiger lily vase which I designed in 1946.

With my father's death I was thrown in at the deep end. Apart from running the factory I was suddenly confronted with the routine art work of producing all the working drawings, from which the tube liners applied the decoration to the ware. This left me little time for creative work.

My main aim was to continue the production of Moorcroft Pottery and prove that I could do it. I have often thought that I might have achieved more spectacular results with outside help, which was even suggested at one point by Arthur Liberty, but by my assessment at that time that would not have been Moorcroft.

I have decided that it was a mixture of dedication and bloody mindedness which drove me to do everything myself.

The ensuing years can be divided roughly into five periods.

1945-1952 The Euphoric Period

Everyone at home and abroad was crying out for colour and supplies after the austerity of war, so Moorcroft was top of the bill. During this period orchid, anemone, autumn leaf, spring flowers and African lily were the mainstay of our production, with an avid demand for any of these decorations in the flambé colours.

In 1947 I designed a few pieces of the early columbine from flowers grown in my garden. This should not be confused with the complete range which I did many years later in the early 1980's. Between 1949 and 1950 I did my first hibiscus piece from pressed flowers sent over from Jamaica, and from the same source bourgainvillaea.

1950s The House and Garden Period

The Festival of Britain in 1951 had a marked effect on the 1950s, which I call the "House and Garden" period or the period of the anodised wastepaper basket - crimson - black - or emerald green. "Contemporary" was the magic word and Scandinavian the magic style. An advertisement by a Longton China manufacturer illustrated a Coffee Set described as "Contemporary Queen Anne".

The design pundits frowned on Moorcroft but we still had good business abroad especially in Canada, where some of my best pieces were sold as lamp bases. The traditional designs continued, but I developed the clematis and hibiscus in ever increasing variety, with individual pieces of wild arum and freesia, with flambé as the source of outstanding variation.

Between 1956 and 1960 we demolished two of our three bottle ovens and completed the transition from coal to electric firing, with the exception of the flambé kiln which continued until 1970.

The finer control of temperature paved the way for new colours, the first of which, a pale yellow background was a completely new departure for Moorcroft.

I have to end my reference to the 1950s on a solemn note because it is relevant to what followed.

In 1956 my first wife died suddenly with a tumour on the brain and for some time I felt that I was pushing the factory not running it.

In 1959 I married Liz, who was very young, very artistic and an inspiration. She still is.

1960s The Transitional Period

In 1961 we ended our long-standing financial connection with Liberty and Co and I became a majority shareholder of the company, which, psychologically made Moorcroft mine as opposed to a legacy from my father.

In production the hibiscus became the most important decoration on an ever increasing variety of shapes and colours.

Other designs were Marine, an underwater fantasy, Caribbean, a suggestion of boats, fish, and islands on a turquoise background, hedgevine from bryony growing in Worcestershire lanes, poplar from a variety of leaves gathered on the golf course, Leaves in the Wind - just two leaves on a white background. There were also extra pieces in wild arum and tiger lily drawn afresh from different species.

1962 My brother John joined the company and made sales his main responsibility. His arrival was very welcome as I had run the factory singlehanded for seventeen years.

1963 Saw the end of production of our Blue Porcelain after 50 years as it was no longer economically viable.

1965 Saw the end of throwing and the change to casting and jolleying, but everything continued to be finished on the turners lathe.

In 1968 I made my first trip to America and Canada. Having studied their furnishing styles, I realised that we had to make a complete break from the blues and pinks, which dominated so many Moorcroft Designs.

The result was coral hibiscus, a coral coloured flower, with sepia centre on an olive green background. To get the balance of colour I required, I re-drew the whole hibiscus range with bolder flowers and less detail than the earlier pieces. Success was immediate especially in Canada and the United States.

From the point of view of the Moorcroft Collectors Club the most significant transition of the 1960s was the change in recognition of early Moorcroft from secondhand pottery to a parity with antiques.

With the end of the 60s came the end of our flambé firing owing to the change from coal gas to natural gas in 1970, as natural gas would not give the required atmosphere in the kiln. I am pleased to say that over the last 18 months under pressure from Hugh I have started again and have had some interesting results.

1970s The Zenith

I describe the 1970s as the Zenith because they combined recognition with very successful trading. In 1971 I made a North American trip including Bermuda where I found coral hibiscus growing wild in my exact colouring. I also had the inspiration for Bermuda lily - the white lily on olive green.

In San Francisco on the same trip I formed the idea for the Moorcroft Shop. The Cannery on Fisherman's Wharf was a rough brick building restored for the display of merchandise against rough brick walls with a patio scene outside. On my return we restored the bottle oven, cleared the surrounding space, landscaped the outside, painted the factory Californian sand colour and opened the shop in November 1971.

In 1972 an exhibition to commemorate the centenary of the birth of my father was held at the Victoria and Albert Museum. This filled a large gallery and a substantial part of the display went on a tour of provincial museums during the following year.

In 1973 there was the Richard Dennis Exhibition at the Fine Art Society, New Bond Street with the Richard Dennis catalogue, which up to that time was the most complete record of Moorcroft covering the period 1897-1973.

1975 was Magnolia year. I made my first drawing at Hodnet Hall in Shropshire in May 1975, and showed my first collection in February 1976. It gave me great satisfaction that within 18

9 *Walter Moorcroft at the Blackpool Trade Fair in 1961, with an unusual display stand he had designed himself. The Pottery Gazette for March commented that: 'the stand formed a natural focal point of interest,' and that the new Caribbean series 'created favourable impressions'*

10 *John Moorcroft and Walter Moorcroft at an exhibition in Paris in September 1963*

11 *The Moorcroft stand for the British Industries Fair of 1953, designed by David Macaulay Advertising*

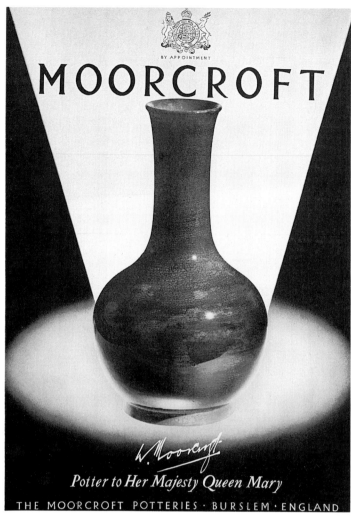

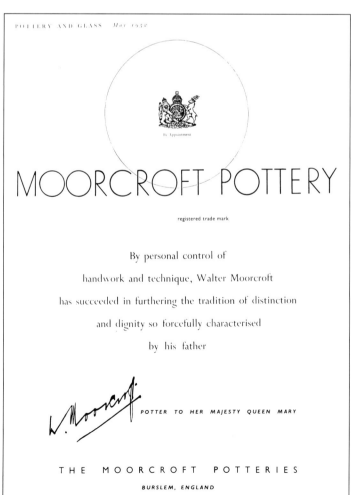

12, 13, 14 Moorcroft have long been noted for their distinctive and adventurous advertising, particularly in trade journals such as Pottery and Glass, and Walter has taken care to maintain the tradition established by his father in the 1930s

months the magnolia had been sold in all five continents. In the late 1970s the Mitsukoshi Corporation had a large promotion of Magnolia and in 1979 the Ato Gallery of Tokyo collected early Moorcroft in London for an exhibition in Japan. I certified each piece as genuine.

1980s – Rough Seas
The 1980s can be called Rough Seas.
This decade started as the 1970s ended on the crest of a wave. Sales to Canada were maintained and even increased despite the effect of the strong pound, and in the summer of 1981 I made a most enjoyable trip to British Columbia as the guest of the Henry Birks Organisation making personal appearances in Victoria and Vancouver. As the outcome of this trip I designed the range of miniature boxes. Six shapes, four flowers and a variety of colours provided a miscellany of well over 100 different pieces.
1982–83 – Recessions in both Canada and Britain meant trouble. The number of workers employed in the industry was reduced by almost a third and a number of factories closed.
In 1984 we were approached by the Churchill Group who are the largest private manufacturers of mass produced earthenware in Stoke-on-Trent and were seeking diversification. This came as a lifeline, and the company was re-structured. My brother John became Managing Director and I was left in charge of design. In the interest of standardisation a large proportion of our designs and shapes were discontinued. After two years Churchill had had enough and despite a very cordial relationship, they expressed their wish to sell out.

After various negotiations Hugh and Richard who had already started production of a new book on Moorcroft stepped in, and, in the analogy of rough seas towed us into harbour for a refit.

After my 70th birthday in February 1987 I officially retired and Richard's wife Sally took over full responsibility for design. We had a party to celebrate the occasion and toasted the New Era which I am sure you will agree has already made most successful progress.

Many improvements have been made at the factory, but the most spectacular development was the opening of the Moorcroft Museum, a fantastic achievement.

Walter Moorcroft Designs, 1946–1988

Spring flowers
William Moorcroft's 1930s design continued in occasional production until the late 1950s, virtually unaltered.

Orchids
Developed by William in c1937, and continued intermittently by Walter through the 1940s and 1950s on blue, green and flambé. Last used in 1972 for special vases made to celebrate the centenary of William's birth, with yellow and blue grounds. The anemone design was also used.

Clematis
Developed by William in 1938/9 from a flower he picked in his drive at home and continued by Walter from 1946 to 1975. Production finally ceased in 1983, except for special orders. Made on dark blue, woodsmoke, green, yellow, ivory and with flambé, and experimentally on turquoise in 1959.

Anemone
William's pre-war design was used regularly by Walter from 1945 until 1975 when he redrew it. The new design was made first on blue and woodsmoke, on yellow from 1978 and green and ivory from 1984.

Fuschia
William's design was used on lampbases for the American market and was a mainstay of production during the war. Production was continued by Walter until c1947, for the Crest Company of Chicago.

Columbine
Walter's first independent design, drawn in 1947 from flowers picked in his garden. This was confined to a few pieces only until the early 1980s when he designed a complete range. It was used first on blue grounds, later on yellow, ivory, green and woodsmoke.

Hibiscus
Drawn c1949 from pressed flowers sent to Walter from Jamaica. Early versions of the design include buds, dropped in the early 1960s, and leaves shaded pink, later replaced by yellow. Coral hibiscus, with its one-colour flower, was introduced in 1968. In 1971 the design was redrawn in Bermuda, and this new range included coral on ivory from 1974, and pink on ivory, green, woodsmoke, yellow and blue. In 1979/80 pink and coral on brown were added, and in 1986 a pale blue and dark blue version was produced, influenced by contemporary furnishing styles.

Bourgainvillaea
Drawn in c1950 from pressed flowers sent to Walter from Jamaica, and used on ivory and green until the early 1960s.

Lilies
The tiger lily was drawn when he was at school in c1935, but the design was not used until c1950 and then remained in occasional production. He redrew it in a different style in the early 1960s. His arum lily was the result of persistent searches in local hedgerows and was produced in greater numbers from 1959 to 1962.

Dianthus and Fresia
Drawn in 1955 and used in small quantities on small vases, trays and bowls, on pearl, ivory and green grounds, over the next couple of years. A turquoise was used experimentally.

Leaves in the Wind
Drawn in 1960 from leaves found by Walter in the lanes of Worcestershire, this restrained design was conceived with flower arranging in mind. It was well received but was withdrawn in 1962 as many retailers found it untypical.

Dahlia
Drawn in 1960 and used experimentally for a short period.

Caribbean and Marine
Originally designed in 1961 to fulfil an order for tankards from a company in Bermuda, this colourful pattern was also used on vases and trays. It was withdrawn in c1963. Similar in style was the marine design, an underwater pattern featuring seahorses, fish and seaweed in bright colours, made between 1962 and 1964.

Poplar Leaves
Drawn in 1962 from leaves collected by Walter at the local golf course, the design was used only on a large vase, with ivory, smoky blue and flambé autumn grounds. About 25/30 made in all.

Poinsettia
The design was drawn in 1967 for a Christmas plate commissioned by Woodward of Vancouver but never went into production.

Maize
Drawn in 1967, the design was produced experimentally to fulfil an order from T Eaton, a Canadian retailer, but never achieved full production.

Bermuda Lily
Drawn by Walter in Bermuda in 1971. After an initial trial with a turquoise ground, he developed the design with a white flower on olive green. Later variations were a yellow flower on ivory (Eastern Lily) in 1975 and a yellow flower on brown (Jungle Brown Lily) in 1978.

Alamander
Drawn by Walter in Bermuda in 1971, the design was used only on about 20/30 small boxes.

Pansy Nouveau
Introduced in 1972 for the American market, the design was inspired by William's pansy design of 1911. The pale green ground and the style of drawing tried to capture the flavour of the Art Nouveau period. It was withdrawn in 1973.

Magnolia
Drawn in 1975 from magnolias seen by Walter in the grounds of Hodnet Hall, Shropshire, and first exhibited in February 1976. Pink flowers on blue were first used, but later ivory, yellow, and olive green grounds were added. This design was being sold in all five continents within 18 months of its inception.

Wild Rose
Drawn for Liberty to be part of a promotion to launch the Mini Metro in September 1980, the design was made experimentally on woodsmoke and pale yellow but never went into production.

Butterfly Bramble and Butterfly Bluebell
Designed in October 1984, these two new patterns were specially produced to appeal to the Moorcroft collector. The third design in the series featured an arum lily drawn with grasses.

Geranium and Campanula
Drawn in Crete in October 1984, these patterns were designed for relatively large scale production, using casting rather than slip trailing. The moulded range also included mugs decorated with a bottle oven, and with single sprays of rose, daffodil, bluebell, and thistle, as well as geranium and campanula.

Tulip
Conceived originally as coloured flowers on a white ground, for use on a lamp, the white tulip design was inspired by some flowers Walter saw on the Royal Copenhagen stand at the 1986 Birmingham Spring Fair. It was subsequently issued on a green ground as a limited edition.

Chestnut Leaves and Pineapple Plant
The pineapple was sketched in Minorca, while the chestnut was drawn one lunchtime at Swinnerton. Both designs were issued as limited editions in 1986.

Anemone
Following Walter's retirement in February 1987, he was invited in 1988 to redraw the original anemone design, and the new range was issued in 1989.

1 Vase decorated with a lily design, showing both sides of the flower, with a light flambé glaze. Drawn by Walter directly from the flower, and dated 1952. Height 14½ ins

2   3

2 Lamp base decorated with an orchid design under a rich flambé glaze, c1954. Height 18½ ins
3 Vase decorated with an anemone design under a flambé glaze, c1954. Height 10½ ins
4 Lamp base decorated with a fuchsia design under a yellow flambé glaze, made for the Crest Company of Chicago, c1948. Height 12 ins
5 Vase decorated with the hibiscus design, the tropical colours emphasised by the flambé glazes, dated 1952. From a small group of about 25, some of which were made for a Cunard cruise liner. Height 10 ins

4   5

1

1 Group of wares decorated with an arum lily design, showing the development of the design into the darker colours of flambé firing, c1960. Black bowl diameter 10 ins

2 Group of wares decorated with various flower designs under flambé glazes, left to right, dahlia bowl 1960, clematis vase designed by William but executed by Walter c1948, clematis dish and small vase 1960, orchid *Laelia Autumnalis* dish 1960. Largest dish diameter 10 ins

2

3

3 Group of wares decorated with the hibiscus design, showing the varied effects of the flambé firing including the turquoise and brandy flame affects achieved by firing close to the limit, 1954-1965. Taller vase height 10¼ ins
4 Group of wares decorated with various flower designs under flambé glazes, left to right, clematis dish 1963, poinsettia Christmas plate 1967, one of 12 trials for a Canadian order, anemone vase c1955, two columbine vases 1954 (taller) and 1948. Christmas plate diameter 10 ins

4

1 Group of wares decorated with a bourgainvillaea design, showing naturalistic colours c1955 and flambé effects 1950 (the vase) and 1960. Plate diameter 10ins.

2 Walter Moorcroft plate decorated with a version of the bourgainvillaea design on a blue ground, c1955. Diameter 10 ins

3 Group of wares decorated with marine and Caribbean designs under rich flambé glazes, 1960-64. Tankard height 3½ ins

4 Group of wares decorated with versions of the clematis design on different ground colours, drawn by William in c1938 and developed by Walter between 1946 and 1975. The jar and cover is dated 1948, the green and ivory ground vase 1956. Tallest vase height 8½ ins

5 Group of wares decorated with an orchid design, drawn by William in 1937 and developed by Walter from c1947. Trumpet vase 1948, flambé dish 1959, yellow and blue ground vases made in 1972 to celebrate the centenary of William's birth, with special backstamp. Dish diameter 10ins

6 Group of wares decorated with Walter's version of his father's spring flowers design, 1947-1957. Tallest vase height 12½ ins

4

5

6

1

1 Group of wares decorated with a columbine design, the squat blue/green vase 1947, the pale flambé vase 1949, the others c1955. Tallest vase height 7½ ins
2 Group of wares decorated with a columbine design showing various ground colours, c1980-1985. The tall green ground vase is from a limited edition of 100, made 1982-1983. Ginger jar height 6½ ins

2

3

3 Vase decorated with an early version of the hibiscus design, showing the leaves shaded with pink and the bud which was dropped from the design in the early 1960s, c1950. Height 12 ins

1 Group of wares decorated with early versions of the hibiscus design, showing different colour ways, left to right, box and cover 1960, plate 1965, small bowl 1949, larger bowl 1955, vase 1962. Box and cover diameter 6ins
2 Group of wares decorated with the hibiscus design on brown and yellow grounds, 1975-1985. Plate diameter 10ins

3

3 Group of wares decorated with the coral hibiscus design, showing green, brown and ivory grounds, 1968-1980. The dish and the adjacent vase on the left were made in limited editions of 100 each in 1982 and 1983. Dish diameter 10¹/₂ ins
4 Group of wares decorated with the hibiscus design on green, woodsmoke, ivory and dark blue grounds, c1974. Tallest vase height 8¹/₂ ins

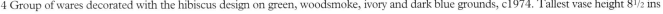

4

1

2

1 Pale and dark blue version of the hibiscus design, introduced 1986 and withdrawn in 1988
2 Two vases decorated with an anemone design, showing the continuation by Walter of his father's pre-war design, c1949. Larger vase height 9½ ins
3 Group of wares decorated with the new version of the anemone design developed by Walter from 1975, showing green and ivory grounds, c1984. Largest vase height 8 ins

3

4

4 Group of wares decorated with Walter's version of the anemone design, showing blue, woodsmoke and yellow grounds, c1975-1980. Ginger jar height 6½ ins

5 Group of wares decorated with various flower designs, left to right, clematis on green, one of about 50 produced in 1959, dianthus on pearl, one of about 100 made on various pale grounds c1955, African lily on box and cover c1953, fresia c1955, clematis on an experimental turquoise 1959. Turquoise vase height 5 ins

5

1 Group of wares decorated with the arum lily design, showing green and ivory grounds, 1959-1962. Vase height 11 ins
2 Group of wares decorated with the arum lily design, showing yellow and blue grounds, and a small planter with a flambé glaze, 1959-1962. Larger dish diameter 8½ ins

3

3 Group of wares decorated with the Leaves in the Wind design, showing the slight decoration and subdued colours chosen with flower arranging in mind, 1960-1962. Largest vase height 8½ ins
4 Group of wares decorated with the Caribbean and marine designs, showing the characteristic bright colours and the exotic fish, 1960-1965. Vase height 9½ ins

4

1

2

3

1 Group of wares decorated with the Pansy Nouveau design, drawn by
Walter for the American market in 1972 and inspired by his father's
pansy design of 1911, 1972-1973. Vase height 11 ins
2 Group of wares decorated with the Bermuda lily design, showing the
green and ivory grounds, introduced in 1973 and 1975. Tallest vase
height 12½ ins
3 Group of wares decorated with the Bermuda lily design, showing the
yellow flower on a brown ground introduced in 1978, and the turquoise
ground produced experimentally in 1971. The vase on the left is from a
limited edition of 200 produced in 1983. Plate diameter 10 ins
4 Vase decorated with a poplar leaves design in autumnal colours,
showing the ivory ground. Small numbers were also made with smoky
blue grounds and with flambe glazes. Dated 1962. Height 12¾ ins

4

1 Group of wares decorated with the magnolia design, showing the dark blue and ivory grounds, c1976. Plate diameter 10½ ins
2 Group of wares decorated with unusual colour versions of the magnolia design, showing its development from 1975. The box and cover with a pale flower on woodsmoke was one of the first trials and is dated 12/5/75. The regular ground colours were dark blue, ivory, lemon yellow and, occasionally, olive green. Planter height 9 ins

3 Three vases decorated with new butterfly and arum lily designs, showing butterflies combined with brambles and bluebells and the lily with grasses, produced in small quantities with collectors in mind from 1984. Height 8 ins

4 Group of wares decorated with experimental designs, left to right, maize vase made in 1967 for T. Eaton of Canada but never fully produced, wild rose plate made on yellow and woodsmoke in 1980 but never produced, tiger lily bowl and plate c1965 and alamander box and cover made in 1971. Vase height 12 ins

1 Group of lamp bases decorated with hibiscus, anemone and clematis designs on dark grounds, c1978. Largest height 12 ins (without light fitting)
2 Publicity photograph showing a range of pendants, brooches and a ring decorated with hibiscus and clematis designs, c1978. The teardrop pendant was also made with lily and magnolia designs. Round pendant diameter 3 ins
3 Group of wares showing blue campanula and pink geranium designs introduced in 1985. These wares featured moulded raised designs rather than hand drawn slip-trailing, but with hand-painting. Yellow and coral campanula were added to the range in 1986. All moulded wares are unsigned. Lamp base height 9½ ins

4

5

6

4 Group of small coasters decorated with a range of designs showing familiar patterns in unusual colours, including Bermuda lily, arum lily and hibiscus, as well as experimental patterns such as maple leaf, 1955-1975. Diameter 5 ins
5 Group of small shaped boxes and covers decorated with standard designs in a range of colour ways, originally inspired by papier maché boxes from Kashmir. Introduced in 1981/2, the range included 110 items. The diamond and clover shapes were dropped in 1984/5. Average diameter 3 ins
6 Set of card trays decorated with standard patterns, designed for bridge players in 1972, and now out of regular production, and four miniature vases which continued the tradition established by Walter's father. Now out of regular production, these miniatures were made from the early 1970s with a range of standard designs on blue, green, ivory, woodsmoke and yellow grounds. Average height 2 ins

Chapter Six
Commemorative Wares

Commemorative wares were made by William Moorcroft at Macintyre's and at Cobridge, and the tradition has been continued by Walter. Moorcroft commemoratives were either adaptions of existing patterns, with inscriptions added, or were specially designed to celebrate a range of public and private events. Their most characteristic feature is a distinctive style of lettering, hand-drawn in slip, perhaps seen at its best on the wide range of mugs produced for occasions such as the coronations of Edward VII and Queen Alexandra, George V and Queen Mary, Edward VIII, and George VI and Queen Elizabeth. The ending of the First World War was also commemorated in this way. Commemorative vases, bowls, jugs, pipe trays and complete tea services were also made. The earliest commemorative piece may have been a two-handled mug inscribed 'Christmas & New Year Greetings' and made in about 1902, one of a number of private commissions, several of which came from Mr & Mrs Lasenby Liberty. Heraldic decoration was also popular, notably on a range

of match holders made for various Oxford and Cambridge colleges. Another long-standing feature of Moorcroft production is motto ware. The first references to pieces decorated with applied mottoes, in both Latin and English, occur in the early 1900s, and there are then irregular mentions in factory records until at least 1935. Many of the motto wares may have been special commissions.

Walter Moorcroft has produced his own range of commemoratives, celebrating the coronation and jubilee of Queen Elizabeth II. He has also made Year plates in limited editions from 1982 to 1986, and year bells from 1983.

1 Group of commemorative mugs, left to right, coronation of Edward VII, 1902, designed by Lasenby Liberty and made for Mr and Mrs Liberty, coronation of George V 1911, made for Mr and Mrs Liberty, First World War, 1919, inscribed 'Their name liveth for evermore', First World War 1919, made for Lady Liberty, George V silver jubilee 1935, coronation Edward VIII 1937, coronation George VI 1937. Height 3½- 4½ ins
2 Group of commemorative wares, left to right, First World War vase 1919 with flambé glaze, George V silver jubilee vase 1935, Edward VIII coronation box and cover 1937, George VI coronation bowl 1937 with flambé glaze, George VI coronation box and cover 1937. White vase height 8 ins

3

4

5

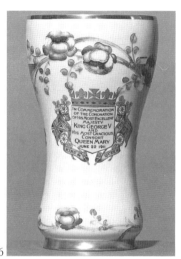

6

7

8

9

3 Norton mug, decorated with a printed patriotic hymn and made for Lord Norton to celebrate the coronation of George V, 1911. Height 4½ ins
4 Powder blue match holder printed with the arms of Kings College Cambridge, c1910. Height 2½ ins
5 Edward VIII Coronation flambé beaker. Height 4½ ins
6 Vase decorated with rose garlands, gilding and a printed panel celebrating the coronation of Georve V, 1911. Height 8 ins
7 Two-handled vase decorated with an heraldic lion, other devices and a Latin inscription, c1911. Height 4½ ins
8 Jug made to celebrate the coronation of Georve VI, 1937. Height 6½ ins
9 Tea service made to commemorate the coronation of George VI and Queen Elizabeth, 1937. Teapot height 5½ ins

1 Vase and bowl made to celebrate the coronation of Queen Elizabeth II, 1953, both made in small limited editions. Vase height 6 ins
2 Year bells made in 1983, 1984, 1985 and 1986 intended to be produced in limited editions of 1000 each, but in the event no more than 500 of each were produced
3 Year plate for 1982 made in a limited edition of 200. Year plates for 1983, 1984, 1985, 1986 and 1987 made in limited editions of 250, and a plate made to celebrate the silver jubilee of Queen Elizabeth II in 1977 in a limited edition of 125. Diameter 8^{1}/$_{2}$ ins

1 W. John S. Moorcroft

By July 1986 it had become clear that the Roper Brothers' plan to take Moorcroft into the volume market was not going to work. They were unwilling to invest more money in the company, and so John Moorcroft was forced to look for other ways to secure the pottery's future. He sought help from Hugh Edwards, a friend and a leading Moorcroft collector who is a partner in Richards Butler, a firm of international solicitors based in the City of London. Edwards, with considerable experience of the ceramic industry gained through some of his clients, notably Norcros plc who own H and R Johnson Tiles Limited, introduced John Moorcroft to tile makers Maw & Company Limited, a Norcros subsidiary and one of the few companies in England still using the slip-trailing technique. However, the very different production and marketing methods used for tiles and decorative pottery meant that the two companies actually had little in common and so, after some delay, Maw's decided not to become involved.

By September the situation had become critical and, with the threat of receivership in the air, the Roper Brothers, having negotiated with two other companies, gave John Moorcroft 48 hours to save the business. He again contacted Hugh Edwards. This time, the approach was more personal, with John inviting Hugh and his wife Maureen to take on the business as partners. With Hugh fully committed to Richards Butler and with Maureen running a busy local law firm in Essex, they decided, after 24 hours careful deliberation, that they did not have enough time to become involved with Moorcroft on their own. So, with 24 hours left, Hugh contacted his old friend Richard Dennis, a dealer in 19th and 20th century ceramics and for years a Moorcroft specialist and, following lengthy discussions

between Hugh and Maureen and Richard and his wife Sally, they decided to act together to try to save Moorcroft and all it stood for, believing that a team comprising a leading Moorcroft dealer, an important Moorcroft collector and the son of the founder as Managing Director might be able to pull the business back from the brink.

On 16 September 1986 Hugh and Maureen Edwards and Richard and Sally Dennis signed an agreement to purchase the Roper Brothers' 70% stake in the company, plus a further 6% from John Moorcroft's shareholding to give them absolute control, leaving 24% of the shares in the hands of John and his wife Gill. Although Hugh Edwards, as a director of many companies, had considerable financial and commercial experience, Moorcroft's other new owners were, to some extent, innocents in the industrial jungle, and their joint decision to buy the company had been inspired more by sentiment and a sense of history than by business acumen. However, all the partners were united by their enthusiasm for pottery, and for Moorcroft in particular. Richard Dennis, who had worked for Sotheby's from 1959 to 1965, and who is well known for his exhibitions and publications about ceramics and had mounted a major Moorcroft exhibition at the Fine Art Society's Bond Street Gallery in 1973. In addition, he had gained some experience of the ceramic industry from his own small pottery, the Dennis China Works. However, it is fair to say that the partners' collective experience had hardly prepared them for the realities of the crisis that faced them at Moorcroft and they found they had to move quickly if their new investment was to stay alive. Although they had, on Hugh Edward's advice, given no guarantees, they quickly realised that their moral commitment, to the Bank, to the staff, to the retailers, to Moorcroft, and to history itself was, in effect, far more binding, and so they set to work to bring Moorcroft back to life.

The problems they inherited included a loyal but demoralised workforce, a decaying factory, disinterested retailers and a lack of marketing initiative. There was a critical need to introduce new designs at the next International Spring Fair, the ceramic industry's major trade show held at the National Exhibition Centre at Birmingham in early February. There had been no significant new Moorcroft designs since the introduction of the magnolia range in 1975 and the market was crying out for something new. From the Ropers' experience, the partners knew that Moorcroft could not be moved down market, and so they were left with only one option, namely to try to rebuild Moorcroft's former reputation for quality and individuality. From the moment of the Edwards and Dennis takeover, it had always been the intention that Sally Dennis should be Moorcroft's new Art Director. Trained at Walthamstow School of Art and later in the Fashion School at the Royal College of Art, where she gained a Des. R.C.A. with a Silver Medal, Sally Tuffin (as she then was) had enjoyed a considerable reputation as a fashion designer. The Foale & Tuffin shop was a famous style leader in London's Carnaby Street during the 1960s and 1970s, and her wide experience of design enabled her to bring to Moorcroft a fresh approach that did not alter in any significant way the distinctive style long associated with the pottery. With everyone working flat out, and with Hugh Edwards keeping the Bank at bay, Moorcroft were able to go to the Spring Fair with six new designs. Three were by Sally, the stylised rose, violet and banksia patterns, and three by Philip Richardson, the art master at the Friends School, Saffron Walden, Essex where, by a strange coincidence, Sally herself had once been a pupil. These, Fairy Rings, Reeds at Sunset and Honeycombe, were more traditional in their approach. Together, the new designs were used to test the market, and to measure the response of both retailers and collectors conditioned by years of exposure to traditional Moorcroft designs such as anemone, hibiscus and magnolia. At the same time new shapes were introduced, some designed by the studio potter Roger Michell and others brought back from earlier periods of production. A design competition was also held at the factory, promoted originally to encourage the staff to play a more active role and rely more on their own initiative. Both Hugh Edwards and Richard Dennis had long been enthusiastic followers of the philosophies of William Morris, who believed that employees should be able to enjoy the fruits of their labour and participate in their own destiny. Pride in individual, high quality work is now actively encouraged and from the outset of the new era staff became involved in the decision-making process. The partners were, therefore, pleased when the competition produced three new designs, dragon by mould maker Trevor Critchlow, fruit and vine by Marjorie Kubanda and ivy by Wendy Mason. Walter Moorcroft also made an important contribution to the design revival with his pineapple, chestnut, tulip, maize and wild arum limited edition patterns, produced prior to his retirement in February 1987.

Following this design explosion, 1987 became a year of consolidation as the Moorcroft name began to re-establish its rightful place in the retail market. Moorcroft pottery made its way back onto the shelves of major retailers such as Selfridge's, Lawley's, and, more important for historical reasons, Liberty's. In May 1987 the first edition of this book was launched at a special Liberty exhibition of Moorcroft old and new, and the links between the two companies, stretching back nearly 90 years, were rebuilt. In Australia Philip Allen, a new Moorcroft Agent in 1986, established this once important market, and Dave Simmons did the same in Canada. Major efforts were also made to build sales in the United States and Japan.

At the same time, as the retailers' confidence increased and the collector market expanded, the resulting cash flow enabled an extensive programme of repairs to begin to bring the factory up to date without in any way altering its unique qualities. The regular floods and leaks started to become a thing of the past, the lavatories, apparently untouched since 1913, were modernised and the bottle oven was restored, winning in the process a National Heritage Award. The value of the past is now fully recognised, and care is taken to rediscover and preserve the fine techniques used by William and Walter in earlier decades. Traditional methods of design, manufacture and decoration are

carefully maintained as these are seen to hold the key to Moorcroft's future. The partners were also aware from the outset that John Moorcroft's contribution was to be vital, for he is uniquely placed to lead the sales drive by promoting his family name all over the world, by attending trade fairs and retailers' special events, by giving lectures and by generally organising publicity to enhance the Moorcroft name.

During 1988 and 1989 a more settled design policy was established, with Sally Tuffin producing a number of new patterns based on a birds and fruit theme. Finches, with its dark blue ground and deliberate parallels with pomegranate, proved to be the most popular. Her other designs have included a pattern based on a William Morris fabric made initially for Sanderson and now sold world wide, tulips, introduced in 1989 and peacock feathers, originally a Liberty exclusive. She had also produced a number of special and limited edition designs featuring polar bears, balloons, penguins, ships, owls and elephants. New designs introduced in 1990 included Spring Blossom and limited editions to celebrate the 50th anniversary of the English Morris Ring in Thaxted and the 600th anniversary of Thaxted Guildhall.

The new ideas that brought Moorcroft back from the brink in the late 1980s have been consolidated during the early 1990s, with the emphasis on satisfying both retail and collector markets. For the former, there has been a steady expansion of the Moorcroft range, with both new patterns, and new colourways for existing patterns. For the traditionalists, Walter Moorcroft has continued to expand his redrawn anemone design. At the same time, Sally Tuffin's new designs, such as Cluny and Rainforest, have broken new ground while remaining distinctly Moorcroft in both style and technique. Sally has demonstrated the flexibility inherent in Moorcroft with these ranges which fit into the much loved landscape tradition while avoiding the temptation simply to revive and recreate. Her new designs have also brought her closer to William's roots in the Macintyre era. Like William, she has given particular emphasis to the art of fitting the pattern to the pot. Increasing stylisation in the William manner allows the pattern to be readily adapted to fit the contours of the shape. Colours have become stronger, richer and much more varied, with increased layering during the painting stages to enhance interest in both the design itself and the ground against which the design is shown. Her energy in pushing back the frontiers of colour limitation has meant that the factory colour palette has been trebled in size. New shapes have been introduced, based largely on those favoured by William. Today, the design philosophy is both more demanding and more experimental, with ranges either planned at the outset in their entirety, or developed gradually from one particular design on one shape. Market forces are, as ever, the determining factor, with the Birmingham trade fairs the key to shape and design development. The period has also seen the return of other former favourites of the William era, for example the decorative teawares and expanding ranges of small vases so attractive to the collector. Even more important have been the new clockcases, inspired by one of William's early clocks deriving inspiration from the Archibald Knox designs for Liberty. Table lamps have also increased in importance, their appeal broadened by the decision to mount them on plinths and an increasing ambition of buyers to have Moorcroft in their homes as useful adjuncts to home furnishing.

Overseas markets are now a powerful component in Moorcroft's new stability, with the emphasis on Australia and New Zealand. John Moorcroft is a regular visitor to these and other markets and his personal appearances at trade fairs and other retail events are the vital backbone that supports Moorcroft's pattern of continued growth. Japan is also a growing market, and during

2 The enlarged decorating shop, 1992.

3 The Moorcroft Museum, opened in 1989 by the late Arnold Mountford. The collection is displayed in the original oak cabinets made by Liberty for the Moorcroft stand at the Wembley Exhibition 1924. In the foreground is the new oak archive table, made by Graham Colyer, and inset with Moorcroft tiles.

a recent trade fair in that country HRH the Duke of Kent visited the Moorcroft stand, reviving traditional Moorcroft links with the Royal family. As with any other manufacturing industry in Britain, export markets play an important role.

Equally vital to Moorcroft's future are the particular interests of collectors at home and abroad, and there has been a steady expansion of limited edition and special issue wares. Most unusual in this field has been the vase made to celebrate the Silver Jubilee of the Sultan of Brunei. New are the annual visitation vases, only available for sale during special shop events, demonstrations, lectures and other special events. All Moorcroft wares now carry a date stamp, with a symbol indicating the year of manufacture, along with increased use of decorators' marks and monograms. Pattern deletion is also faster and more formalised and many designs made in the late 1980's and subsequently withdrawn are now finding their place in the secondary collector market. Some Collectors seek out the work of particular decorators, while Wendy Mason's special colourways of standard designs have an individual appeal. Personal interest and enthusiasm are the watchwords for both the Moorcroft staff, and for the thousands of collectors worldwide.

The primary vehicle for this is the Moorcroft Collectors Club launched in 1987 and now enjoying a thriving and expanding membership. The Club has a regular colour magazine and a busy programme of special events, the most important of which is the annual collectors' weekend and open day, held at the factory during the summer and attended by several hundred members. A highlight of the Collectors' weekend each year is the auction of unique pieces individually coloured by the paintresses. Club members, and Moorcroft collectors generally, are always given a warm welcome at the factory shop. Adjacent is the Moorcroft Museum, opened in 1989 by the late Arnold Mountford, with a remarkable display of Moorcroft wares of all periods housed in the original oak display cabinets first made by Liberty's for the Moorcroft stand at the Wembley Exhibition of 1924. The continually expanding displays have been augmented by the Moorcroft archive, a vital study collection of documents and other material which can be seen by appointment.

Moorcroft, its staff, its designs and its history all enjoy a high profile today. This unique factory is increasingly appreciated throughout the world as a centre of excellence, where a concern for the highest standards in traditional handcraft techniques is without equal in the British ceramic industry. The distinctive qualities of Moorcroft Pottery, and the Moorcroft traditions of design and manufacture still echo the philosophies of William Morris, so important to William Moorcroft at the start of his career and hopefully will continue to do so into the future.

Production

1

2

3

4

5

6

7

8

9

10

1 Trevor Critchlow, chief mould maker modelling a teapot and his assistant, Paul Pointon, checking a mould
2 Andrew Tunnicliffe, apprentice turner and maker, releasing a mould and Janet Kirkland jollying a coaster
3 Peter Ryan turning and his wife, Pauline, fettler and sponger, impressing the Moorcroft stamp
4 Justin Emery, Works Manager, loading the biscuit kiln
5 Bernard Bayley, dipper, with Lynn his wife and assistant
6 Robert Churchill, packer, and Olive Leake, the selector, in the glost warehouse
7 Steven Swann, the Northern salesman, with the office staff Beverley Potts and Barbara Laidler
8 Shop manageress, Kim Plant, and assistant Michele Reeves
9 Gill Moorcroft, Collectors Club secretary
10 HRH The Duke of Kent with Sally Tuffin, Moorcroft Designer, and Richard Dennis at Life Style Europe, Tokyo, 1992
11 Hugh Edwards, Chairman of W. Moorcroft PLC, and his wife Maureen

11

Decorating

1

2

3

4

5

6

7

8

9

10

11

1 Preparation of tracings: Sandra Eaton with Elizabeth Smith inking a bramble and a finch design
2 The 27ins. carp team: Sue Pointon, Gillian Powell and Marjorie Hill
3 The Rain Forest team: Gillian Leese, Sharon Austin, Wendy Mason, Hayley Mitchell
4 A Cluny team: Marie Penkethman, Jayne Hancock, Mary Etheridge
5 A Mamoura team: Jenny James, Gwyneth Hibbitt, Julie Dolan
6 A finch team: Barbara Mountford, Sue Gibbs, Shirley Lowndes
7 A cat plate team: Ailie Woodhead, Lorraine Knowles, Jackie Moores
8 A bramble team: Alison Neale, Beverley Wilkes, Sylvia Abell
9 A violet team: Karen Gibson, Hayley Smith, Paula Nixon
10 A magnolia team: Alisa Phillips, Catherine Beech, Mandy Dobson, Maggie Thompson
11 An anemone team: Shirley Anderson, Debra Hancock, Sally Bailey

The decorators work in teams with responsibility for particular patterns. However, the photographs do not always portray complete teams as the ranges require larger teams. As a result, there is some flexibility among the teams

Walter Moorcroft Designs

1

1 Group of wares introduced late 1986, from left to right: The wild arum design produced in an edition of 50 7 ins vases. The pineapple plant produced on a 14½ ins vase, and a planter, in an edition of 100 each. The chestnut leaves design produced on 12 ins and 14½ ins vases both with brown or ivory backgrounds, and a 9 ins tray of the same design and colourways (not illustrated), all made in editions of 50
2 Group of wares introduced late 1986, from left to right: The magnolia design, originally introduced in 1975, this special edition of 20 12 ins vases has an olive green ground. The tulip design introduced in 1985 as a small edition of lamps on an ivory ground, and re-introduced in an edition of 50 on an olive green ground, divided among a 10 ins vase, 7 ins vase and a 10 ins plate. Also produced with yellow tulips on blue, and pink tulips on blue, each in an edition of 50 10 ins plates, and 7 ins and 10 ins vases for Canada. The maize design originally introduced in the late 1960s as a lamp base for T. Eaton & Co. of Canada, but not put into production. Only a few trial vases were made. The 1986 edition numbers 100 12 ins vases

2

3

4

3 A commemorative plate designed by the staff and presented to Walter Moorcroft on his retirement in February 1987. 14 ins

4 An experimental revival of flambé undertaken by Walter Moorcroft from 1987. 14 ins

5 & 6 The anemone range, redrawn by Walter Moorcroft in 1989 and currently made in three colours with yellow, green and blue grounds. The yellow and green versions were withdrawn in 1991. Two handled vase 13 ins, plate 10 ins

5

6

Staff Designs

1

1 A group of wares decorated with the dragon design in three colours. Designed by Trevor Critchlow and introduced in 1987. The white ground withdrawn 1989 and the blue ground in 1990. The tallest vase 10 ins

2

2 A group of wares decorated with the fruit and vine design by Marjorie Kubanda, biscuit ware selector (formerly paintress). The vase, produced for the Australian and Canadian markets, was also made for Liberty's as a lamp base with a green ground. The planter produced in an edition of 500 from 1986, the 8 ins plate made in an edition of 75 for Showplace of Melbourne, Australia in 1989. A further 50 were also made without the Showplace backstamp

3

4

3 Vase and bowl decorated with the ivy design by Wendy Mason and Julie Dolan, introduced and withdrawn in 1987. Vase 7 ins

4 The dragon design was also used in the three colourways on the 27 ins vase

Philip Richardson Designs

1

1 Group of wares decorated with the Fairy Rings design introduced 1987 and withdrawn 1990, showing pale green and dark green grounds. Tallest vase height 14 ins

2 Group of wares decorated with the honeycomb design introduced in 1987, withdrawn 1989. Tallest vase height 10 ins

2

3

5

3 Group of wares decorated with the Reeds at Sunset design, introduced in 1987 and withdrawn in 1990. Tallest vase height 12 ins

4 Large vase decorated with the Heron design introduced 1988, and the related charger. The vase height 27 ins

5 In 1991 the Fairy Rings design was renamed Toadstool, and issued in this new colourway. Withdrawn at the end of 1991. Taller vase height 12 ins

4

Sally Tuffin Designs

1 Sally Tuffin, Moorcroft Designer
2 Vase decorated with a Moorcroft name, produced experimentally in several colourways in 1987. Height 6½ ins
3 Group of wares decorated with the rose design introduced in 1987, and withdrawn in 1991, made initially in a variety of colours and then from 1988 made only with the red rose. Height of vase 10 ins

1

1 Group of wares decorated with the violet design, introduced 1987, and withdrawn 1990. Height of vase 10 ins
2 Group of wares decorated with the banksia design, made primarily for the Australian market, introduced in 1987, and withdrawn in 1990. The left-hand vase, the earlier version, 7 ins

2

3

3 Group of wares decorated with the wattle design, introduced in 1988 initially for the Australian market, withdrawn 1990. Height of the candlestick 8 ins
4 Group of wares decorated with the plum design, introduced in 1988 and withdrawn in 1990. Height of tallest vase 12 ins

4

1

2

3

4

1 Group of wares decorated with the lemon design introduced in 1988 and withdrawn in 1990. Height of tallest vase 12 ins
2 Group of wares decorated with the sunflower design, introduced in 1988. The more stylised design on the 27 ins vase
3 Group of wares decorated with the peacock design, introduced in 1988 and made initially for Liberty's. Withdrawn 1990. The tallest vase 12 ins
4 Large 27 ins vase decorated with the finches design on the blue ground introduced 1989

1

1 Group of wares decorated with the finches design on the blue ground, introduced in 1988. Charger 14 ins diameter
2 Group of wares decorated with the finches design on the ochre ground, introduced in 1989 and withdrawn in 1990. Height of tallest vase 12 ins

2

3

3 Group of wares decorated with the tulip design, introduced in 1989. Height of tallest vase 12 ins
4 Group of wares decorated with the spring blossom design introduced in 1990 and withdrawn in 1991. Height of tallest vase 14 ins

4

1

1 Two vases decorated with an adaptation of the William Morris design called Golden Lily by J. H. Dearle. Introduced in 1989 in conjunction with Sanderson's. Height 12 ins. A new colourway and a new shape ware introduced in January 1991. For details see page 184
2 Set of six saki cups, commissioned in 1988 by Ato Galleries of Tokyo in an edition of 500 sets. Height 2 ins
3 Vase decorated with the orange design introduced in 1989 and withdrawn in 1990. Height 10 ins
4 Group of wares decorated with the robins design introduced 1988 and withdrawn in 1991. Height of vase 5 ins

2

3

4

5

5 Group of wares made initially to commemorate the Australian bicentenary of 1988, and depicting the First Fleet with HMS Sirius, and subsequently made for a wider market. Covered jar, edition of 25. Charger, editions of 100 for Australia and 150 worldwide. Vase, editions of 100 for Australia and 150 worldwide. Height of vase 14 ins

6 Vase decorated with a rampant lion design, commissioned in 1988 by the Lion's Den, Moorcroft Dealers of Leamington Spa, and made in an edition of 50. Height 10 ins

7 Vase decorated with the eagle owl design, introduced in 1988 in an edition of 500. Height 12 ins

6

7

1

2

1 Vase decorated with a polar bear design, introduced in 1988 in an edition of 250 for the Canadian market. Height 6½ ins
2 Vase decorated with an elephant design. Commissioned in 1989 by Thomas Goode to celebrate the centenary of their Minton showroom elephants and introduced in an edition of 25. Height 13 ins
3 Groups of wares decorated with a penguins design, introduced in 1989 in limited editions, the vase 350 and the plate 150 each. Diameter of plate 10 ins. Painted by Sue Gibbs and Julie Dolan

3

4

5

4 Vine plate made in 1990 for Selfridges, London, in an edition of 50. Diameter 10 ins. The edition was painted by Wendy Mason
5 Charger decorated with a hot air balloon design commissioned by R. & R. Collectibles in 1988 in an edition of 200. Diameter 14 ins
6 Group of wares decorated with the swan design, 10 ins plate and vase introduced in 1990 and made in an edition of 350 each
7 A bowl decorated with the Temptation design introduced in 1990 and produced in a limited edition of 500. $10^1/_2$ ins diameter

7

6

Sally Tuffin Designs: New Colourways and Extended Ranges

1 A group of wares decorated with the carp design. The two-handled vase introduced the design in 1990, and the range was expanded in 1991. Dish diameter 14 ins

2 A group of wares, adaptations of William Morris designs (see page 180), decorated with Golden Lily and Autumn Flowers. Left, Autumn Flowers introduced in 1992. The two Golden Lily vases were introduced in 1989. The Golden Lily charger was introduced in 1991, and is also made with a white ground. Vase height 12 ins

3 Vase decorated with the carp design. Introduced in 1991 as an addition to the carp range and produced in a limited edition of 100. Height 28 ins

1

2

3

4

1 Group of wares decorated with the finch design in the green colour-way, introduced in 1991 and withdrawn at the end of 1992. Tallest vase height 10 ins

2 Group of wares decorated with the violet design with new dark blue ground, introduced 1992. Diameter of plate 10 ins

3 Group of wares decorated with the finch design, with the new teal green ground, introduced 1993. Tallest vase height 10 ins

4 Two vases decorated with the tulip design in the black colourway, introduced in 1991 and withdrawn in 1992. Larger vase height 10 ins

5 Group of wares decorated with the robin design, in the blue colour-way introduced in 1991 and withdrawn in 1992. Diameter of plate 8 ins

5

Sally Tuffin Designs: New Ranges

1

1 Group of wares decorated with the bramble design, introduced in 1991. Tallest vase 10ins
2 Group of wares decorated with the buttercup design, introduced in 1991. Tallest vase height 16 ins. This design was first made as a year plate for 1990

2

1992 saw the introduction of a number of related designs that revived the Moorcroft tradition of landscape decoration, a theme first exploited by William in the early Florian version of Hazledene. Inspiration came from a variety of sources, including the mythology of the Middle East (Mamoura), medieval tapestry (Cluny), the threatened species of the Rain Forest, and the Seasons.

3 Group of wares decorated with the Mamoura design, introduced in 1992. Tallest vase height 16 ins
4 Group of wares decorated with the Cluny design, introduced in 1992 and extended 1993. Tallest vase height 10 ins.

1

2

1 Group of wares decorated with the Rain Forest design, introduced 1992, and extended in 1993. The plants depicted include Cattleya, Violacea, Acacallis Cyanea. Tallest vase height 12 ins

2 Vase decorated with another Rain Forest design, produced in 1993 in a limited edition of 100 for Michael and Kate Trim, franchisees of the Body Shop International, with profits donated to help save the Brazilian rain forest. Height 7 ins

3 Vase decorated with the Rain Forest design, introduced in 1992 in a limited edition of 150 incorporating the three flowers from the range with the addition of Distictella, Neoregelia Eleutheropetala, Heliconia Chartacea and Streptocalyx Poeppigii. A donation of £3000, a percentage of the selling price, was made to the Rain Forest Foundation by W. Moorcroft PLC. Vase height 16¹/₂ ins

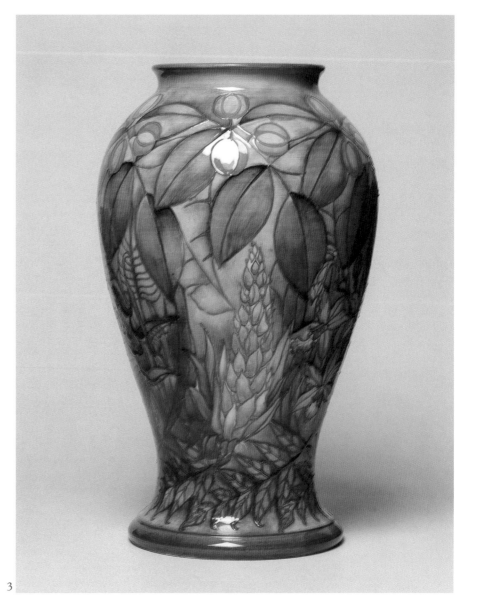

3

4 Group of wares decorated with the lattice design, introduced in 1992. This, the most stylised of the new landscape designs, follows the William Moorcroft tradition of allowing the shape of the pot to determine the geometry of the pattern. Taller vase height 8 ins

5 Vases decorated with the Seasons design, left, summer, right winter. Taller vase height 6 ins

6 Teawares decorated with the violet design, introduced 1991. The sets consist of teapot, sugar bowl, cream jug and cup and saucer

7 Cups and saucers from the teaware range, introduced in 1991, showing the four patterns, buttercup, bramble, green finch and violet

4

5

6

7

Sally Tuffin: Special Designs and Limited Editions

1

2

1 A group of wares decorated with the Tudor Rose design. A 5 ins vase produced in two colourways in 1992 in editions of 100 each; an 8 ins plate produced in 1991 in an edition of 100 and painted by Katherine Lloyd; and the blue Tudor Rose Special Events vase for 1992. The first Special Events vase, produced in 1991, was a 5 ins green finch vase

2 Two vases decorated with the dandelion design. The 5 ins vase produced in 1991 in an edition of 250 and the 8 ins vase introduced in 1992 and made in an edition of 200, both commissioned by Neville Pundole, 20th Century Antiques, Norfolk

3 An 8 ins plate decorated with the Pohutukawa design, produced in 1992 in an edition of 220, and a 5 ins vase made in an edition of 100 in 1990, commissioned by Tanfield Potter, Auckland, New Zealand

4 Two 5 ins vases decorated with the Gothic Windows design made in editions of 100 in each colourway, for exclusive sale at the Collectors Showcase event held in London in 1991

3

4

5

6

5 Vase decorated with the blue gum design, introduced 1993 in a limited edition of 500 for the Australian market. Height 7ins. A 16$\frac{1}{2}$ ins vase with the blue gum design will be made during 1993 in an edition of 50, also for the Australian market.
6 Covered box and vase decorated with blue, yellow and pink roses, introduced 1993, and produced in a limited edition of 500 each.
Height of vase 10 ins
7 The Windsor carnation vase, produced in a limited edition of 300 exclusively for Talents of Windsor in 1993. Height 11 ins
8 The cat plate, produced in 1992/3 in an edition of 300 for Richard Dennis, London. Diameter 10ins

7

8

1

2

1 Plate made in 1991 in a limited edition of 500 to commemorate the move after 300 years of Spitalfields Market, London, to a new site at Temple Mills. A plate was presented to HRH the Duke of Gloucester at the official opening. Diameter 8 ins

2 8 ins vase made in 1992 in a limited edition of 65 to commemorate the Silver Jubilee of the reign of His Majesty Duli Yang Maha Mulia Paduka Seri Baginda Sultan Haji Hassanal Bolkiah Mu'zzaddin Waddaulah. Designed by Sally Tuffin from the artwork of Maimuna Mohamad, the vase displays the Sultan's palace, Istana Nurul Iman, viewed from the Brunei River, framed by the rainforest vegetation.

3 Shakespeare ginger jars made in 1991 and 1992 in limited editions of 250 each, exclusively for B & W Thornton of Stratford-on-Avon. Left, A Midsummer Night's Dream, right, Ophelia.

4 Two 8 ins plates from a proposed series of three, made in 1989 and 1991 in limited editions of 500 each for the Thaxted Guildhall Trustees. Left, Thaxted Guildhall, right, John Webb's Windmill.

5 Group of wares made exclusively for members of the Moorcroft Collectors Club. Centre, the grapevine vase 1987/88; left, the daisy vase 1988/89; right, the rose jug 1990. Daisy vase height 7 ins

6 Wares made exclusively for members of the Moorcroft Collectors Club. Left, the sweet pea vase for 1991, centre, the nasturtium ginger jar for 1992, right, the fuchsia vase for 1993. Sweet pea vase height 10 ins

3

4

5

6

1

2

3

4

5

1 Year plates for 1988, 1989 and 1990 made in editions of 250 each. Diameter 8 ins
2 Year plates for 1991, 1992 and 1993, made in a limited edition of 500 each. Diameter 8 ins
3 Selection of wares with standard designs painted in 1988 and 1989 in unique colours for the auction held at the annual Collectors Club weekend. Each is marked CC with the date. Diameter of plate 10 ins
4 & 5 Since 1991, Sally Tuffin designs have been issued in small quantities with individually painted colourings by Wendy Mason. Above, the blossom design; below, the sunflower jug, and a group of wares decorated with a new rose pattern introduced in 1992 specially for this purpose

Miscellaneous Designs

1

2

3

1 A selection of lamp bases decorated with a range of recent designs

2 A selection of clocks decorated with current designs. The shape is based on a William Moorcroft clock case inspired by a design for Liberty's by Archibald Knox. Height 6 ins

3 A selection of new small shapes introduced in 1993 to extend the existing ranges, decorated with current patterns. Smallest vase height 4 ins

4 Two vases decorated with current designs on a new shape inspired by an early Moorcroft vase first used at Macintyres, introduced in 1993. Height 11 ins

5 A group of wares decorated with Walter Moorcroft's magnolia design in the new wine colourway, introduced exclusively for Australia in late 1991, released generally in 1992. Diameter of plate 10 ins

4

5

1 Vase decorated with a dinosaur design, introduced in 1988 in an edition of 300, initially for the North American market. Height 9¹/₂ ins

2 The Abbots Bromley Chalice, decorated with symbolic images designed by Joe Hobbs and the Thaxted Morris Men, and made in 1991 in a limited edition to celebrate 50 years of dancing in 'The Morris Ring' at Thaxted. Height 10 ins

3 Peter the Pig introduced in 1990, modelled by Roger Mitchell and decorated with the Temptation design

4 Group of mugs, from the top, the robin mug, the bottle oven mug made for the First National Garden Festival, Stoke-on-Trent (1986), the Beaufort House mug made for Richards Butler 1989, the Moorcroft Museum mug 1989, the Thaxted Morris Men mug 1987, the spring blossom mug, the rose hip mug, the blackberry mug, the plum mug, the magnolia mug. The last four were made initially for Liberty's in 1990, 1989, 1988 and 1987.

5 Mugs designed by Sally Tuffin with colourings by Wendy Mason, made exclusively for sale during Open Weekends organised by the Collectors Club in 1991 and 1992, showing the factory bottle oven and the members marquee.

Chapter Eight

Signatures and Backstamps

Moorcroft pottery can be marked in a number of ways, all of which can be a help with identification and dating. These can include the Moorcroft signature or initials, printed or impressed factory marks, retailers' marks, design registration numbers, and pattern or shape marks. Paper labels with printed factory marks were also widely used. Precise dating is generally quite difficult, and the details of the design and decoration can often provide more clues than the marks. Important pieces sometimes carry dates, and many wares produced during the period of transition from the Washington works to the new Cobridge factory, 1912-1914, are dated. Otherwise, it is a matter of relying on familiarity with style and marks to select the likely period of manufacture.

Signatures and Initials

From the start, William Moorcroft established the habit of signing or initialling wares made under his control in his department at Macintyre's, as a mark of quality. A signature never meant that he had made or decorated the piece himself. Several styles were used during the Macintyre period, the full painted signature, *W Moorcroft des.* (designer), painted initials, *WM des.* or an incised signature or initials. Later Macintyre wares were signed without the des. Signatures during this period are generally in green, but other colours can be found. Pieces from the Cobridge period are generally signed in blue from c1918 but this is not a firm rule. The colour of signature was determined more by the brush that came to hand than by any planned system of dating. Wares made to Moorcroft's designs but not in his department, such as the printed Aurelian Wares and the Dura tablewares, were rarely signed. At Cobridge the signature or initials became bolder, larger and more stylised.

When he took control of Cobridge in 1945, Walter Moorcroft established the tradition of initialling all wares over about five inches in height or diameter. Although his style of initials is similar to his father's, they can be distinguished from each other, particularly by association with the design used. Until the early 1980s Walter only signed new designs or important pieces in full, but recently the full signature has been used more frequently, particularly on wares made with collectors in mind. Before 1959 Walter used a blue/grey colour which changed to green after that date. From 1978 brown was generally used, reverting to green in about 1981.

Unless stated otherwise in the captions, all the wares illustrated in this book carry some form of painted or incised Moorcroft signature or initials.

Factory Marks

Macintyre art wares carry some form of printed factory mark. The pre-Moorcroft wares, Washington Faience, Taluf ware and Gesso Faience all had individual printed backstamps, and this pattern was followed by Moorcroft's Florian Ware, Butterfly Ware and Hesperian Ware. When the Florian Ware mark was given up in about 1905, it was replaced by a standard printed Macintyre monogram backstamp, used on its own, or combined with a retailer's mark. At the Cobridge factory, Moorcroft began to use impressed marks and this pattern has been continued to the present day. There have been two main styles, the simple factory name and the facsimile signature and Royal mark used from 1928. Marks printed with a rubber stamp have been used on small pieces, and printed and painted marks have also been used on recent limited editions.

Retailers' Marks

Moorcroft wares often carry printed retailers' marks as this was a service available at the Macintyre factory at a small extra cost. About twenty retailers have been noted, the most important of which was Liberty. From the early 1900s Florian and other wares were made for Liberty and marked accordingly. From about 1906 many pieces carried only the Liberty mark and the Moorcroft signature. The other distinctive backstamp was the Hesperian Ware made for Osler's. Some retailer's marks were painted, for example those on wares made for Shreve of San Francisco. Retailers' marks were rarely used during the Cobridge period until 1986, since then many have been printed, some for overseas customers.

Design Registration Numbers

It was common practice at the Macintyre factory to register both shapes and designs at the Patent Office and many Moorcroft-designed shapes and patterns were registered between 1898 and about 1905 in the Macintyre name. Printed registration numbers were often included with the backstamp, giving an indication of the date of introduction of the pattern or shape, but not the date of manufacture.

Pattern and Shape marks

Impressed or painted numbers with an M prefix can often be found on many Macintyre wares, a continuation of a shape and pattern identification system in use at the factory before Moorcroft's arrival. The working of the system is not entirely clear. At Cobridge impressed shape numbers were regularly used. Decorators' and gilders' marks can also be found.

Paper Labels

A rectangular paper label was used from the early 1920s. The circular paper label was introduced after the award of the Royal Warrant in 1928 and continued in use in various forms until the Warrant lapsed in 1978. A label printed in red was used on seconds.

1 Gesso Faience mark, printed in brown on wares designed by Harry Barnard from c1897. Continued in occasional, or accidental, use until the early 1900s and so can be found on Moorcroft designs

2 Florian Ware mark printed in brown, 1898-c1905 and early painted Moorcroft signature

3 Florian Ware mark printed in brown, 1898-c1905, printed design registration mark, early incised Moorcroft initials and painted pattern or shape number

4 Butterfly Ware mark printed in brown, c1900 and incised Moorcroft initials

5 Osler's Hesperian Ware mark printed in brown, c1901-3 and painted Moorcroft signature

6 Standard Macintyre factory mark printed in brown, c1904-1913, printed design registration mark, painted initials and painted pattern or shape number

7 Standard Macintyre factory mark printed in brown, c1904-1913, printed retailer's mark, painted signature and impressed shape number

8 Liberty mark printed in green, c1903-1913, Liberty paper label, painted signature, and impressed shape number. Painted Liberty marks can also be found

9 Stamped Tudric mark, used on Moorcroft wares made for Liberty and mounted with hammered pewter, c1916-1923

10 Painted signature usually with a date, used at the new Cobridge works from October 1913 to January 1914. No impressed marks

11 Impressed Cobridge factory mark 1914-1916, impressed date (only found for 1914) and shape number M46. n.b. Many impressed shape numbers lack and letter M

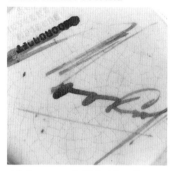

12 Impressed Cobridge factory mark, c1916 and painted signature. ENGLAND was added to comply with international tariff regulations

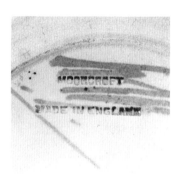

13 Impressed Cobridge factory mark c1918-1929 and painted initials. BURSLEM is omitted and MADE IN ENGLAND was added to comply with USA import regulations

14 Impressed Cobridge factory mark MOORCROFT. MADE IN ENGLAND 393 c1918-1926, painted signature, printed Moorcroft paper label, printed Liberty paper label (Retail). From 1926-1928 similar impressed marks are found but without an impressed shape number due to the change from a treadle lathe to a power driven lathe

15 Impressed factory mark with facsimile signature and POTTER TO HM THE QUEEN, 1928-1949, painted signature and printed paper Royal Warrant label, in use 1928-1953. n.b. Paper label changes to POTTER TO HM QUEEN MARY in 1936, following the death of her husband King George V. See mark number 16

16 Impressed factory mark with facsimile initials, painted Walter Moorcroft signature 1945-1949 and printed paper Royal Warrant label

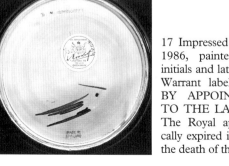

17 Impressed factory mark, c1949-1986, painted Walter Moorcroft initials and later printed paper Royal Warrant label, in use 1953-1978. BY APPOINTMENT POTTER TO THE LATE QUEEN MARY. The Royal appointment automatically expired in 1978, 25 years after the death of the Queen

18 Impressed factory mark, c1949-1986 and painted Walter Moorcroft signature

19 Recent painted Walter Moorcroft signature and date

20 Impressed factory mark 1986-present, painted monogram of William John Moorcroft and impressed *arrow* for 1990

21 Impressed factory marks and *candlestick* for 1992. Painted mark S.T. DES, found on large vases designed by Sally Tuffin 1987-1993, painted signature of William John Moorcroft found on some large vases

22 Impressed factory marks and *bell* for 1991. Painted monogram of William John Moorcroft and S.T. DES with **W** PINXIT found on pots with specially painted colourways by Wendy Mason

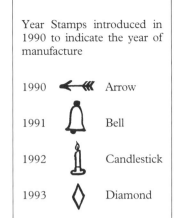

Year Stamps introduced in 1990 to indicate the year of manufacture		
1990	←◀◀◀	Arrow
1991	🔔	Bell
1992	🕯	Candlestick
1993	◇	Diamond

SPECIAL MARKS

23 Printed mark used in 1972 on wares made to commemorate the centenary of William Moorcroft's birth. This mark was used on six different shapes

24 Painted Walter Moorcroft initials and printed marks used in the early 1980s to indicate the number of pieces produced of a pattern on the same shape and size and made in a particular year. (Used only on 9¹/₂ ins – 14 ins vases and 8 ins and 10 ins bowls). The oval printed mark commemorates the 90th anniversary of Tasmanian retailers E.A. Joyce and Son

25 Printed mark used on miniature vases in the 1970s

26 Printed mark found on pots made exclusively for members of the Moorcroft Collectors Club

27 Impressed factory mark and *candlestick* for 1992, and painted mark M.C.C. 92. found on pots with special colourways made for the annual Moorcroft Collectors Club auction

Moorcroft Marks 1986-1993

The Moorcroft tube liners and paintresses formerly used impressed and painted letters of the alphabet and symbols to mark their work. Since late 1986 they have used personal monograms. These are shown below, together with the dates of employment.

TUBE LINERS

Gillian Powell	ℊℙ	1977 – present
Ailie Woodhead	A𝒲	1987 – present
Alison Neale	A/	1988 – present
Gillian Leese	Cₙ	1985 – present
Shirley Lowndes	ⅇ	1955 – present
Karen Gibson	Kℊ	1989 – present
Katherine Keeling	kₖ	1988 – 1989
Marie Penkethman	ℳℙ	1990 – present
Catherine Beech	R.	1992 – present

PAINTRESSES

Name	Mark	Dates
Wendy Mason	W	1979 – present
Hayley Mitchell	Hₐ	1987 – present
Margaret Nash	₥𝒩	1968 – 1991
Sue Gibbs	ℊ	1961 – 1975, 1984 – present
Angela Scoffins	ℊ	1974 – 1992
Mary Etheridge	ℳₑ	1961 – 1968, 1987 – present
Jayne Hancock	ℋ	1987 – present

Continued on following page

PAINTRESSES

Hayley Smith	1988 – present		Marjorie Hill	1987 – present
Sue Pointon	1970 – 1979,		Jackie Moores (Degg)	1988 – present
	1988 – present		Beverley Wilkes	1989 – present
Jennifer James	1987 – present		Katherine Lloyd	1988 – 1992
Janet Kirkland	1989 – present		Adrienne Wain	1947 – 1964,
Lily Gwynne	1945 – 1954,			1987 – 1992
	1956 – 1960,		Paula Nixon	1990 – present
	1989 – 1991		Sylvia Abell	1991 – present
Lynn Ford	1984 – 1988		Lisa Phillips	1991 – present
Julie Dolan	1980 – present		Jackie Norcup	1992 – present
Sandra Eaton	1987 – present		Sian Leeper	1992 – 1993
Gwyneth Hibbitt	1956 – 1970,		Jackie Moores	1988 – present
	1973 – present		Shirley Anderson	1992 – present
Barbara Mountford	1958 – 1966,		Sally Anne Bailey	1992 – present
	1987 – present		Susan Gwyneth Clarke	1992 – present
Sharon Austin	1987 – present		Elizabeth Smith	1992 – present
Mandy Dobson	1987 – present		Lorraine Knowles	1992 – present
Julie Rushton	1988 – present		Maggie Thompson	1992 – present
Christine Brundrett	1977 – 1989			

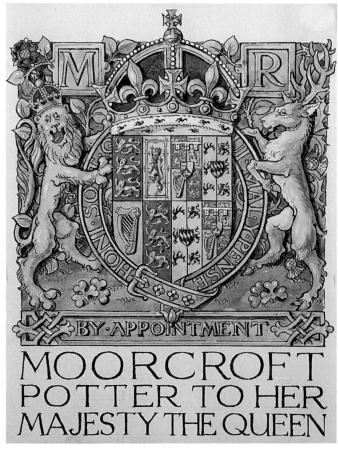

Original watercolour design for the Royal coat of arms added to the
Moorcroft exhibition stand after the award of the Royal Warrant

Index

Designs 1986-1993

Staff Designs:

Philip Richardson Designs:

Sally Tuffin Designs

Miscellaneous Designs:

Pre-war factory shard tip mosaic, made and designed by Candace Bahouth and unveiled by the late Arnold Mountford on 15th June 1991. The mosaic is sited on the wall of the factory shop.